A demonstration of the being and attributes of God: more particularly in answer to Mr. Hobbs, Spinoza, and their followers. ... Being the substance of eight sermons preach'd at the cathedral-church of St. Paul, in the year 1704

Samuel Clarke

A demonstration of the being and attributes of God: more particularly in answer to Mr. Hobbs, Spinoza, and their followers. ... Being the substance of eight sermons preach'd at the cathedral-church of St. Paul, in the year 1704. ... By Samuel Clark, ...

Clarke, Samuel
ESTCID: T116144
Reproduction from British Library

London : printed by Will. Botham, for James Knapton, 1705.
[16],264p. ; 8°

Eighteenth Century
Collections Online
Print Editions

Gale ECCO Print Editions

Relive history with *Eighteenth Century Collections Online*, now available in print for the independent historian and collector. This series includes the most significant English-language and foreign-language works printed in Great Britain during the eighteenth century, and is organized in seven different subject areas including literature and language; medicine, science, and technology; and religion and philosophy. The collection also includes thousands of important works from the Americas.

The eighteenth century has been called "The Age of Enlightenment." It was a period of rapid advance in print culture and publishing, in world exploration, and in the rapid growth of science and technology – all of which had a profound impact on the political and cultural landscape. At the end of the century the American Revolution, French Revolution and Industrial Revolution, perhaps three of the most significant events in modern history, set in motion developments that eventually dominated world political, economic, and social life.

In a groundbreaking effort, Gale initiated a revolution of its own: digitization of epic proportions to preserve these invaluable works in the largest online archive of its kind. Contributions from major world libraries constitute over 175,000 original printed works. Scanned images of the actual pages, rather than transcriptions, recreate the works *as they first appeared.*

Now for the first time, these high-quality digital scans of original works are available via print-on-demand, making them readily accessible to libraries, students, independent scholars, and readers of all ages.

For our initial release we have created seven robust collections to form one the world's most comprehensive catalogs of 18th century works.

Initial Gale ECCO Print Editions collections include:

History and Geography
Rich in titles on English life and social history, this collection spans the world as it was known to eighteenth-century historians and explorers. Titles include a wealth of travel accounts and diaries, histories of nations from throughout the world, and maps and charts of a world that was still being discovered. Students of the War of American Independence will find fascinating accounts from the British side of conflict.

Social Science

Delve into what it was like to live during the eighteenth century by reading the first-hand accounts of everyday people, including city dwellers and farmers, businessmen and bankers, artisans and merchants, artists and their patrons, politicians and their constituents. Original texts make the American, French, and Industrial revolutions vividly contemporary.

Medicine, Science and Technology

Medical theory and practice of the 1700s developed rapidly, as is evidenced by the extensive collection, which includes descriptions of diseases, their conditions, and treatments. Books on science and technology, agriculture, military technology, natural philosophy, even cookbooks, are all contained here.

Literature and Language

Western literary study flows out of eighteenth-century works by Alexander Pope, Daniel Defoe, Henry Fielding, Frances Burney, Denis Diderot, Johann Gottfried Herder, Johann Wolfgang von Goethe, and others. Experience the birth of the modern novel, or compare the development of language using dictionaries and grammar discourses.

Religion and Philosophy

The Age of Enlightenment profoundly enriched religious and philosophical understanding and continues to influence present-day thinking. Works collected here include masterpieces by David Hume, Immanuel Kant, and Jean-Jacques Rousseau, as well as religious sermons and moral debates on the issues of the day, such as the slave trade. The Age of Reason saw conflict between Protestantism and Catholicism transformed into one between faith and logic -- a debate that continues in the twenty-first century.

Law and Reference

This collection reveals the history of English common law and Empire law in a vastly changing world of British expansion. Dominating the legal field is the *Commentaries of the Law of England* by Sir William Blackstone, which first appeared in 1765. Reference works such as almanacs and catalogues continue to educate us by revealing the day-to-day workings of society.

Fine Arts

The eighteenth-century fascination with Greek and Roman antiquity followed the systematic excavation of the ruins at Pompeii and Herculaneum in southern Italy; and after 1750 a neoclassical style dominated all artistic fields. The titles here trace developments in mostly English-language works on painting, sculpture, architecture, music, theater, and other disciplines. Instructional works on musical instruments, catalogs of art objects, comic operas, and more are also included.

old books. new life.

The BiblioLife Network

This project was made possible in part by the BiblioLife Network (BLN), a project aimed at addressing some of the huge challenges facing book preservationists around the world. The BLN includes libraries, library networks, archives, subject matter experts, online communities and library service providers. We believe every book ever published should be available as a high-quality print reproduction; printed on-demand anywhere in the world. This insures the ongoing accessibility of the content and helps generate sustainable revenue for the libraries and organizations that work to preserve these important materials.

The following book is in the "public domain" and represents an authentic reproduction of the text as printed by the original publisher. While we have attempted to accurately maintain the integrity of the original work, there are sometimes problems with the original work or the micro-film from which the books were digitized. This can result in minor errors in reproduction. Possible imperfections include missing and blurred pages, poor pictures, markings and other reproduction issues beyond our control. Because this work is culturally important, we have made it available as part of our commitment to protecting, preserving, and promoting the world's literature.

GUIDE TO FOLD-OUTS MAPS and OVERSIZED IMAGES

The book you are reading was digitized from microfilm captured over the past thirty to forty years. Years after the creation of the original microfilm, the book was converted to digital files and made available in an online database.

In an online database, page images do not need to conform to the size restrictions found in a printed book. When converting these images back into a printed bound book, the page sizes are standardized in ways that maintain the detail of the original. For large images, such as fold-out maps, the original page image is split into two or more pages

Guidelines used to determine how to split the page image follows:

• Some images are split vertically; large images require vertical and horizontal splits.
• For horizontal splits, the content is split left to right.
• For vertical splits, the content is split from top to bottom.
• For both vertical and horizontal splits, the image is processed from top left to bottom right.

A DEMONSTRATION

OF THE

Being and Attributes

OF

G O D:

More Particularly in Anſwer to

Mr. *HOBBS*, *SPINOZA*,

And their Followers.

Wherein the Notion of *LIBERTY* is Stated, and the Poſſibility and Certainty of it Proved, in Oppoſition to *Neceſſity* and *Fate*.

Being the Subſtance of Eight S E R M O N S Preach'd at the Cathedral-Church of St. *Paul*, in the Year 1704. at the Lecture Founded by the Honourable *ROBERT BOYLE* Eſq;

By *Samuel Clark*, M A Chaplain to the Right Reverend Fathei in God *JOHN*, Lord Biſhop of *Norwich*.

Rom. 1. 20. *For the Inviſible things of Him from the Creation of the World, are cleirly ſeen, being undeiſtood by the things that are mide, even his Eternal Power and God-head : So that they aie without excuſe*

London, Printed by Will. Botham, for James Knapton, at the *Crown* in St. *Paul*'s Church Yard. 1705.

TO THE

Most Reverend Father in God

THOMAS

Lord Archbishop of *Canterbury*;
and Primate of all *England* :

Sir *HENRY ASHVRST*, Baronet.

Sir *JOHN ROTHERAM*, Knight,
Serjeant at Law ;

JOHN EVELIN, Esquire ;

Trustees Appointed by the Honourable *ROBERT BOYLE*,
Esquire.

This Discourse is humbly Dedicated.

THE

PREFACE.

THere being already publiſhed many and good Books, to prove the Being and Attributes of God; I have choſen to contract, what was requiſite for me to ſay upon this Subject, into as narrow a Compaſs; and to expreſs what I had to offer, in as few Words as I could with Perſpicuity. For which Reaſon I have alſo confined my ſelf to One only Method or continued Thread of Arguing, which I have endeavoured ſhould be as near to Mathematical as the Nature of ſuch a Diſcourſe would allow: Omitting ſome other Arguments, which I could not diſcern to be ſo evidently

A 3   con-

The PREFACE.

conclusive: Because it seems not to be at any time for the real Advantage of Truth, to use Arguments in its behalf, founded only on such Hypotheses, as the Adversaries apprehend they cannot be compelled to grant. Yet I have not made it my business, to oppose any of those Arguments; because I think it is not the best way for a Man to recommend his own Performance by endeavouring to discover the Imperfections of Others, who are ingaged in the same Design with himself, of promoting the Interest of true Religion and Virtue. But every Man ought to use such Arguments only, as appear to Him to be clear and strong, and the Readers must judge whether they truly prove the Conclusion.

THE

THE
CONTENTS.

A 4   from

The Contents.

Prop.

The Contents.

Of

The Contents.

That

The Contents.

Proved

The Contents.

Of

The Contents.

Of

The Contents.

Of

The Contents.

BOOKS Printed for James Knapton, *at the* Crown *in* St. Paul's Church-Yard.

A Paraphrase on the Four *Evangelists.* Wherein, for the clearer Understanding the Sacred History, the whole Text and Paraphrase are Printed in separate Columns over against each other. Together with Critical Notes on the more difficult Passages, very Useful for Families. In two Volumes. By *Samuel Clarke*, M. A. Chaplain to the Right Reverend Father in God, *John*, Lord Bishop of *Norwich*. Price 12 s.

The whole Duty of a Christian, Plainly Represented in three Practical Essays, on *Baptism*, *Confirmation* and *Repentance*,

pentance. Containing full Instructions for a Holy Life
With earnest Exhortations, especially to young Persons,
drawn from the Consideration of the Severity of the Dis-
cipline of the Primitive Church. The 2d. Edition. By
Samuel Clarke, M. A. Chaplain to the Right Reverend
Father in God *John* Lord Bishop of *Norwich.* Price
stitch'd 6 *d.* Bound 12 *d,* Fine Paper.

Jacobi Rohaulti Physica. Latine vertit, recensuit, &
uberioribus jam Annotationibus ex illustrissimi *Isaaci Neu-
toni* Philosophia maximam partem haustis, amplificavit
& ornavit *Samuel Clarke,* A. M. Admodum Reverendo
in Christo patri, Joanni Episcopo Norvicensi, a Sacris
Domesticis. Accedunt etiam in hac secunda Editione,
novæ aliquot Tabulæ æri incisæ. 8*vo.* Price 8 *s*

Some Reflections on that part of a Book called *Amyntor.*
Or, The Defence of *Milton's* Life, which relates to the
Writings of the Primitive Fathers and the Canon of the
New Testament. *In a Letter to a Friend.* Octavo: Price
6 *d.*

ERRATA.

Pag.	Line		Read
64	15	*in Margin.*	*Ocell. Lucan*
104	9		*impossible*
127	15		*perfection*
204	9		*possibly*
209	18	*in Margin.*	*not inconsistent*
210	12		*to*
221	20		*insisted*
224	22		*protorest*
235	15		*exactly.*

A

A DEMONSTRATION
OF THE
Being and Attributes
OF
GOD:

More particularly in Anfwer to
Mr. *Hobbs, Spinoza,* and their
Followers.

A LL thofe who either *The In-*
are or pretend to be *troducti-*
Atheifts ; who either *on.*
disbelieve the Being of
God, or would be thought to do
fo ; or, which is all one, who
deny the Principal Attributes of
the Divine Nature, and fuppofe

B God

God to be an Unintelligent Being, which acts merely by Neceſſity ; that is, which, in any tolerable Propriety of Speech, acts not
at all, but is only acted upon : All
Men that are *Atheiſts,* I ſay, in
this Senſe , muſt be ſo upon one
or other of theſe three Accounts.

Atheiſm   Either, *Firſt,* becauſe being ex-
ariſes   tremely ignorant and ſtupid, they
from ſtu- have never duly conſidered any
pid Igno- thing, nor made any juſt uſe of
rance ·   their natural Reaſon , to diſcover
.even the plaineſt and moſt obvious
Truths , but have ſpent their time
in a manner of Life very little
Superiour to that of Beaſts.

Or from   Or, *Secondly,* becauſe being to-
groſs   tally debauched and corrupted in
Corrupti- their Practiſe, they have, by a vici-
on of   ous and degenerate Life, corrupted
Manners: the Principles of their Nature, and
defaced the Reaſon of their own
Minds ;

Minds; and inftead of fairly and impartially enquiring into the Rules and Obligations of Nature, and the Reafon and Fitnefs of Things, have accuftomed themfelves only to mock and fcoff at Religion; and being under the Power of E-vil Habits, and the Slavery of Un-reafonable and Indulged Lufts, are refolved not to hearken to any Reafoning which would oblige them to forfake their beloved Vi-ces.

Or, *Thirdly,* becaufe in the way *Or from* of Speculative Reafoning, and up- *falfe Phi-* on the Principles of Philofophy, *lofophy.* the Arguments ufed againft the Being or Attributes of God, feem to them, after the ftricteft and fulleft Inquiry, to be more ftrong and conclufive, than thofe by which we indeavour to prove thefe great Truths.

Thefe

These seem the only Causes that can be imagined, of any Man's disbelieving the Being or Attributes of God, and no Man can be suppos'd to be an Atheist, but upon one or other of these three Accounts. Now to the two former of these three sorts of Men ; namely, to such as are wholly ignorant and stupid, or to such as through habitual Debauchery have brought themselves to a Custom of mocking and scoffing at all Religion, and will not hearken to any fair Reasoning ; it is not my *present* Business to apply my self. The One of these wants to be instructed in the first Principles of *Reason*, as well as of *Religion* : The Other disbelieves only for a present false *Interest*, and because he is desirous that the Thing should not be true. The One has *not yet arrived* to the use of his Natural Faculties : The other has

has *renounced* them, and declares he will not be argued with, as a Rational Creature. 'Tis therefore the third fort of Atheifts only, namely thofe who in the Way of Speculative Reafoning, and upon the Principles of Philofophy, pretend that the Arguments brought againft the Being or Attributes of God, do, upon the ftricteft and fulleft Examination, appear to them to be more ftrong and conclufive, than thofe by which thefe great Truths are attempted to be proved : Thefe, I fay, are the only Atheiftical Perfons, to whom my prefent Difcourfe can be fuppofed to be directed, or indeed who are capable of being reafoned with at all.

Now before I enter upon the main Argument, I fhall premife feveral Conceffions, which thefe

Men,

A Demonstration of the

̉ ̉ ̉ on ̉ ̉ ̉ own Princi-
̉ ̉ ̉ ̉ ̉ unavoidably obliged to
̉ ̉ ̉

In the
very
valuable

And, *First*, they muſt of neceſſity own, that ſuppoſing it cannot be proved to be true, yet at
leaſt 'tis a thing very deſirable, and
which any wiſe Man would wiſh
to be true, for the great Benefit
and Happineſs of Men; that there
was a God, an Intelligent and
Wiſe, a Juſt and Good Being, to
govern the World. Whatever
Hypotheſis theſe Men can poſſibly frame; whatever Argument
they can invent, by which they
would exclude God and Providence out of the World; That
very Argument or Hypotheſis will
of neceſſity lead them to this Con-
ceſſion. If they argue, that our
Notion of God ariſes not from
Nature and Reaſon, but from the
Art and Contrivance of Politicians;
that

that Argument it felf forces them to confefs, that 'tis manifeftly for the Intereft of Humane Society, that it fhould be believed there is a God. If they fuppofe that the World was made by Chance, and is every Moment fubject to be deftroyed by Chance again ; no Man can be fo abfurd as to contend, that 'tis as comfortable and defirable to live in fuch an uncertain State of things, and * fo continually liable to Ruin, without any Hope of Renovation ; as in a World that were under the Prefervation and Conduct of a Powerful, Wife and Good God. If they argue againft the Being of God, from the Faults and Defects which they imagine they can find in the Frame and Conftituti-

* Maria ac Terras Cælumq;
Una dies dabit exitio,
multofq, per annos
Suftentata ruet moles &
machina Mundi.
——Dictis dabit ipfa fidem res
Forfitan, & graviter terrarum motibus orbis
Omnia conquaffari in parvo tempore cernea.
Lucret. Lib. 5.

on

on of the *Visible* and *Material* World;
this Suppofition obliges them to
acknowledge, that it would have
been better the World had been
made by an Intelligent and Wife
Being, who might have prevented
all Faults and Imperfections. If
they argue againft Providence,
from the Faultinefs and Inequality
which they think they difcover in
the Management of the *Moral*
World, this is a plain Confeffion,
that 'tis a thing more fit and defirable in it felf, that the World
fhould be governed by a Juft and
Good Being, than by mere Chance
or Unintelligent Neceffity. Laftly, If they fuppofe the World to
be eternally and neceffarily Self-
Exiftent, and confequently that
every thing in it is eftablifhed by a
Blind and Eternal Fatality; No
rational Man can at the fame time
deny, but that Liberty and Choice,

or

or a Free Power of Acting, is a more eligible State, than to be determined thus in all our Actions, as a Stone is to move downward, by an absolute and inevitable Fate. In a word, which way soever they turn themselves, and whatever Hypothesis they make, concerning the Original and Frame of things : Nothing is so certain and undeniable, as that *Man,* considered without the Protection and Conduct of a Superiour Being, is in a far worse Case, than upon Supposition of the Being and Government of God, and of Mens being under his peculiar Conduct, Protection and Favour. *Man* of himself is infinitely insufficient for his own Happiness : * *He is liable to many Evils and Miseries, which he can neither prevent nor redress : He is full of Wants which he cannot supply, and compassed about*

* Archb. Tillot-son's Sermon on Job 28. 28.

with Infirmities which he cannot remove, and obnoxious to Dangers which he can never sufficiently provide against : He is secure of nothing that he enjoys in this World, and uncertain of every thing that he hopes for : He is apt to grieve for what he cannot help, and eagerly to desire what he is never likely to obtain, &c. Under which evil Circumstances 'tis manifest there can be no sufficient Support, but in the Belief of a Wife and Good God, and in the Hopes which true Religion affords. Whether therefore the Being and Attributes of God can be *demonstrated* or not; it must at least be confessed by all rational and wife Men, to be a thing very *Desirable,* and which they would heartily *Wish* to be true, that there were a God, an Intelligent and Wife, a Just and Good Being, to Govern the World.

Now

Now the use I desire to make of this Concession, is only this : That since the Men I am arguing with, are unavoidably obliged to confess, that 'tis a thing very desirable at least, that there should be a God; they must of necessity, upon their own Principles, be very willing, nay, desirous above all things, to be convinced that their present O-pinion is an Errour, and sincerely hope that the contrary may be de-monstrated to them to be true ; and consequently they are bound with all seriousness, attention and impartiality, to consider the weight of the Arguments, by which the Being and Attributes of God may be proved to them.

Secondly, All such Persons as I am speaking of, who profess them-selves to be Atheists, not upon any present Interest or Lust, but purely upon the Principles of

Scoffing at Reli-gion, in-excusable.

Rea-

Reafon and Philofophy ; are bound
by thefe Principles to acknowledge,
that all mocking and fcoffing at
Religion, all Jefting and turning
Arguments of Reafon into Drol-
lery and Ridicule, is the moft un-
manly and unreafonable thing in
the World : And confequently
they are obliged to exclude out
of their Number, as Irrational and
Self-condemned Perfons, and un-
worthy to be argued with, all
fuch Scoffers at Religion, who de-
ride at a venture, without hearing Reafon, and will not ufe the
Means of being convinced and fa-
tisfied. Hearing the Reafon of the
Cafe with Patience and Unpreju-
dicednefs, is an Equity which Men
owe to every Truth that can concern them, and which is neceffary
to the Difcovery of *every Kind of
Errour :* How much more in things
of the utmoft Importance !

Thirdly,

Thirdly, Since the Persons I am *Virtue* discoursing to, cannot but own, *and good Manners* that the Supposition of the Being *absolutely* of God, is in it self most desirable, *necessary.* and for the benefit of the World, that it should be true ; They must of Necessity grant further, that supposing the Being and Attributes of God, to be Things not indeed Demonstrable to be true, but only *Possible,* and such as cannot be demonstrated to be false ; as most certainly they cannot : And much more, supposing them once made to appear *Probable,* and but more likely to be true, than the contrary Opinion : Nothing is more evident, even upon these Suppositions only, than that Men ought in all Reason to live piously and virtuously in the World ; and that Vice and Immorality are, upon all Accounts, and under all Hypotheses, the most ab-

surd

furd and inexcufable Things in Nature.

Thus much being premifed, which no Atheift who pretends to be a rational and Fair Inquirer into Things, can poffibly avoid granting; (and other Atheifts, I have before faid, are not to be difputed with at all, as being Enemies to *Reafon*, no lefs than to *Religion*, and therefore abfolutely Self-condemned :) I proceed now to the main Thing I at firft propofed to my felf, namely, to indeavour to fhow, to fuch confidering Perfons as I have already defcribed, that the Being and Attributes of God, are not only poffible or barely probable in themfelves, but alfo ftrictly demonftrable to any unprejudiced Mind from the moft unconteftable Principles of Reafon.

And

And here, becaufe the Perfons I am at prefent dealing with, muft be fuppofed not to Believe any Revelation, nor acknowledge any Authority which they will fubmit to, but only the bare force of Reafoning : I fhall not, at this time, draw any Teftimony from Scripture, nor make ufe of any fort of Authorities, nor lay any ftrefs upon any popular Arguments in the Matter before us , but confine my felf to the Rules of ftrict and demonftrative Argumentation.

Now many Arguments there are, by which the Being and Attributes of God have been undertaken to be *Demonftrated* : And perhaps moft of thofe Arguments, if throughly underftood, rightly ftated, fully purfued, and duly feparated from the falfe or uncertain Reafonings, which have fome-
                                   times

times been intermix'd with them, would at length appear to be substantial and conclusive. But because I would endeavour, as far as possible, to avoid all manner of perplexity and confusion, therefore I shall not at this Time use any Variety of Arguments, but endeavour by One clear and plain Series of Propositions necessarily connected and following one from another, to demonstrate the Certainty of the Being of God, and to deduce in order the Necessary Attributes of his Nature, so far as by our Finite Reason we are enabled to discover and apprehend them : And because it is not to my present purpose to explain or illustrate things to Them that Believe, but only to convince Unbelievers, and settle them that Doubt, by strict and undeniable Reasoning ; therefore I shall not allege

allege any thing, which however really true and useful, may yet be liable to contradiction or dispute ; but shall indeavour to urge such Propositions only, as cannot be denied without departing from that Reason, which all Atheists pretend to be the Foundation of their Unbelief. Only it is absolutely Necessary before all Things, that they yield to lay aside all manner of Prejudices ; and especially such, as have been apt to arise from the too frequent Use of *Terms of Art* which have no *Ideas* belonging to them, and from the common receiving certain *Maxims of Philosophy* as true ; which at the bottom seem to be only *Propositions without any meaning or Signification at all.*

C   I. First

Some-
thing
must have
Existed
from E-
ternity.

I. First then, it is Absolutely and Undeniably certain, that *Something has existed from all Eternity.* This is so evident and undeniable a Proposition, that no Atheist in any Age has ever presumed to assert the contrary; and therefore there is little need of being particular in the Proof of it. For since Something Now Is, 'tis manifest that Something always Was: Otherwise the Things that Now Are, must have risen out of Nothing, absolutely and without Cause: Which is a flat Contradiction in Terms: For to say a Thing is produced, and yet that there is no Cause at all of that Production, is to say that Something is *Effected* when it is *Effected by Nothing,* that is, at the same time when it is *not Effected at all.* Whatever Exists, has a Cause of its Existence, either in the Necessity

fity of its own Nature; and then it
muſt have been Eternal: Or in the
Will of ſome other Being; and
then that Other Being muſt, at
leaſt in the Order of Nature and
Cauſality, have Exiſted before
it.

That *Something* therefore *has* *Of the*
really Exiſted from Eternity, is one *Difficul-*
of the certaineſt and moſt evident *ty of Con-*
ceiving
Truths in the World; acknow- *Eternity.*
ledged by all Men, and diſputed
by none. Yet as to the *Manner*
How it can be; there is nothing
in Nature more difficult for the
Mind of Man to conceive, than
this very firſt Plain and Self-evi-
dent Truth. For, *How an Eter-*
nal Duration can Now be actually
Paſt, is a thing utterly as impoſſible
for our narrow Underſtandings to
comprehend, as any thing that
is not an expreſs Contradiction *in*
Terms, can be imagined to be:

and

and yet to deny the Truth of the Proposition, would be to assert *something still far more Unintelligible.*

Difficulties arising merely from the Nature of Eternity, not to be regarded, because equal in all Suppositions.

The use I would make of this Observation, is This. That since in all Questions concerning the Nature and Perfections of God, or concerning any Thing to which the Idea of Eternity or Infinity is joyned; tho' we can indeed Demonstrate certain Propositions to be true; yet it is impossible for us to comprehend or frame any adæquate or complete Ideas of the *Manner How* the Things so demonstrated can Be: Therefore when once any Proposition is clearly Demonstrated to be true; it ought not to disturb us, that there be perhaps perplexing Objections on the other side, which for want of adæquate Ideas of the Manner of the Existence of the Things demonstrated, are not easy to be answered.

Indeed,

Indeed, were it poſſible there ſhould be any Propoſition which could equally be *Demonſtrated* on both ſides of the Queſtion, or which could on both ſides be *reduced to imply a Contradiction*; This it muſt be confeſſed, would alter the Caſe: Upon this abſurd Suppoſition, all Difference of True and Falſe, all Thinking and Reaſoning, and the uſe of all our Faculties, would be entirely at an end. But when to Demonſtration on the one ſide, there are oppoſed on the other, only Objections raiſed from our want of having adæquate Ideas of the Things themſelves; this ought not to be eſteemed a Real Difficulty. 'Tis poſitively and clearly Demonſtrable, that Something has been from Eternity: All the Objections therefore raiſed againſt the Eternity of any thing, grounded merely on our want of

C 3 having

having an adæquate Idea of Eternity ; ought to be looked upon as of no real Solidity. Thus in other the like Instances: 'Tis Demonstrable, for Example, that Something must be actually Infinite : All the Metaphysical Difficulties therefore, which arise usually from applying the Measures and Relations of Things Finite to what is Infinite ; and from supposing *Finites* to be *Parts* of *Infinite*, when indeed they are not properly so, but only as Mathematical Points to Quantity, which have no Proportion at all ; ought to be esteemed vain and of no Force. Again, 'tis in like manner Demonstrable, that Quantity is infinitely Divisible : All the Objections therefore raised by comparing the imaginary *Equality or Inequality of the Number of the Parts of Unequal Quanti-*ties, whose Parts have really *no*

Num-

Number at all, they all having Parts *without Number* ; ought to be lookt upon as weak and altogether Inconclusive : To ask whether the Parts of unequal Quantities be *equal in Number* or not, when they have *no Number at all* ; being the same thing as to ask whether two infinite Lines be equal in length or not, that is, whether they *End* together, when neither of them have *any End at all.*

II. *There has Existed from Eternity Some One Unchangeable and Independent Being.* For since Something must needs have been from Eternity ; as hath been already proved, and is granted on all Hands : Either there has always Existed One Unchangeable and *Independent* Being, from which all other Beings that are or ever were

There must have existed from Eternity One Independent Being.

in

in the Univerfe, have received their Original; or elfe there has been an infinite Succeffion of changeable and *dependent* Beings, produced one from another in an endlefs Progreffion, without any Original Caufe at all : Which latter Suppo-fition is fo very abfurd, that tho' all Atheifm muft in its Account of moft Things (as fhall be fhown hereafter) terminate in it, yet I think very few Atheifts ever were fo weak as openly and directly to de-fend it. For it is plainly impof-fible and Contradictory to it felf. I fhall not argue againft it from the fuppofed Impoffibility of Infi-nite Succeffion, *barely and abfolute-ly confidered in it felf*; for a Rea-fon which fhall be mentioned here-after : But, if we confider fuch an infinite Progreffion, as *One* en-tire Endlefs *Series* of *Dependent* Beings ; 'tis plain this whole *Se-ries*

ries of Beings can have no Cause *from without,* of its Existence ; because in it are supposed to be included *All Things* that are or ever were in the Universe : And 'tis plain it can have no Reason *within it self,* of its Existence ; because no One Being in this Infinite Succession is supposed to be Self-existent or *Necessary* (which is the only Ground or Reason of Existence of any thing, that can be imagined *within the thing it self,* as will presently more fully appear,) but every one *Dependent* on the foregoing : and where *no Part* is necessary, 'tis manifest *the whole* cannot be necessary ; absolute Necessity of Existence, not being an outward, relative, and accidental Determination ; but an inward and essential Property of the Nature of the Thing which so Exists. An infinite Succession therefore of

merely

merely *Dependent* Beings, without
any Original Independent Cauſe ,
is a *Series* of Beings, that has neither Neceſſity nor Cauſe, nor any
Reaſon *at all* of its Exiſtence,
neither *within it ſelf* nor *from
without :* that is, 'tis an expreſs
Contradiction and Impoſſibility ;
'tis a ſuppoſing *Something* to be
cauſed, (becauſe it's granted in every
one of its Stages of Succeſſion, not to
be neceſſarily and from it ſelf ;) and
yet that in the whole it is cauſed *abſolutely by Nothing* : Which every
Man knows is a Contradiction to be
done *in Time* ; and becauſe Duration
in this Caſe makes no Difference, 'tis
equally a Contradiction to ſuppoſe
it done from Eternity : And conſequently there muſt *on the contrary,* of
Neceſſity have Exiſted from Eternity, ſome *One* Immutable and *Independent* Being : Which, what it is, remains in the next place to be in-
quired.   III. *That*

III. *That Unchangeable and In-* The One *dependent Being, which has Existed* Independent Be-*from Eternity, without any external* ing, must *Cause of its Existence; must be* be necessary *Self-existent, that is, Necessarily-* sarily *existing.* For whatever Exists, must either have come into Being out of Nothing, absolutely without Cause; or it must have been produced by some External Cause; or it must be Self-Existent. Now to arise out of Nothing, absolutely without any Cause; has been already shown to be a plain contradiction. To have been produced by some External Cause, cannot possibly be true of every thing; but Something must have Existed Eternally and Independently; as has likewise been shown already. It remains therefore, that That Being which has existed Independently from Eternity, must of Necessity

ty

ty be Self-exiftent.   Now to be
Self-exiftent, is not, *to be Produced
by it felf* ; for that is an expiefs
Contradiction : But it is, (which
is the only Idea we can frame of
Self-exiftence, and without which
the Word feems to have no Signification at all : It is, I fay,) *to
exift by an Abfolute Neceffity in the
Nature of the Thing it felf.*   And
this Neceffity muft be *Antecedent* ;
not indeed in time, to the Exiftence of the Being it felf ; becaufe
That is Eternal *:* but it muft be
Antecedent in the Natural Order of
our Ideas, to our Suppofition of
its Being : That is ; This Neceffity muft not barely be *confequent*
upon our Suppofition of the Exiftence of fuch a Being : (For then
it could not be a Neceffity Abfolutely fuch in it felf, nor confequently the Ground or Foundation of the Exiftence of any thing,
being

being on the contrary only a Confequent of it,) But it muſt *antecedently* force it felf upon us, whether we will or no, even when we
are indeavouring to fuppofe that
no fuch Being Exiſts : The attempting which very Suppofition,
becaufe it is an Impoffible One,
does of all other ways the moſt
clearly evidence to us the Abſo-
luteneſs of this Neceffity, Antecedent to any Suppofition whatfoever : For when we are indeavouring to fuppofe that there is no
Being in the Univerfe that exiſts
Neceffarily ; we always find in our
Minds (befides the foregoing Demonſtration of Something being
Self-exiſtent, from the Impoffibility of every Things being dependent ; We always find in our
Minds, I fay,) fome Ideas, as of
Infinity and Eternity : which to
remove, that is, to fuppofe that there

is no Being in the Univerfe to which thefe Attributes are neceffarily inherent, is a Contradiction in the very Terms. For He that can fuppofe Eternity and Immenfity removed out of the Univerfe, may, if he pleafe, as eafily remove the Relation of Equality between twice two and four.

From hence it follows.

The True Notion of Self-Exift-ence. 1ft. That *the only true Idea of a Self-exiftent or Neceffarily Ex-ifting Being, is the Idea of a Being, the Suppofition of whofe Non-exiftence is an exprefs Contradiction.* For fince 'tis abfolutely impoffible but that there muft be Somewhat Self-exift-ent; that is, which exifts by the Neceffity of its own Nature; 'tis plain, that That Neceffity cannot be a Neceffity confequent upon any foregoing Suppofition, (be-caufe Nothing can be Antecedent to that which is Self-Exiftent, no

not

not its own Will, fo as to be
the Caufe of its own Exiftence,)
but it muft be a Neceffity abfolutely fuch in its own Nature.
Now a Neceffity, not relatively
or confequentially, but abfolutely
fuch in its own Nature ; is nothing elfe, but a plain Impoffibility or Implying a Contradiction
to fuppofe the contrary. For inftance ; the Relation of Equality
between twice two and four, is an
abfolute Neceffity ; only becaufe
it is an immediate Contradiction
in Terms to fuppofe them unequal. This is the only Idea we
can frame, of an Abfolute Neceffity ; and to ufe the Word in
any other Senfe, feems to be
ufing it without any Signification
at all.

If any one now asks, what
fort of Idea the Idea of that Being
is, the Suppofition of whofe Non-
Exiftence

Exiſtence is thus an expreſs Contradiction : I anſwer, 'Tis the Firſt
and Simpleſt Idea we can poſſibly
frame, or rather which (unleſs
we forbear thinking at all) we
cannot poſſibly extirpate or remove
out of our Minds, of *a moſt Simple
Being, abſolutely Eternal and Infinite,
Original and Independent.* For,
that he who ſuppoſes, there is no
Original Independent Being in the
Univerſe, ſuppoſes a Contradiction ; has been ſhown already :
And that he who ſuppoſes there
may poſſibly be no *Eternal* and *Infinite* Being in the Univerſe, ſuppoſes likewiſe a Contradiction, is
evident from hence, (beſides that
theſe two Attributes do neceſſarily follow from Independent Exiſtence, as ſhall be ſhown hereafter :) that when he has done his
utmoſt, in indeavouring to imagine that no ſuch Being Exiſts; he
cannot

cannot avoid imagining an Eternal and Infinite Nothing; that is, he will imagine Eternity and Immensity removed out of the Universe, and yet that at the same time they still continue there.

This Argument, the *Cartesians,* *The Error of the Cartesians.* who supposed the Idea of *Immensity* to be the Idea of mere *Matter,* have been mightily perplexed with. For (however *in Words* they have contradicted themselves, yet in *Reality*) it has been easier for them to be driven even to that most intolerable Absurdity, of asserting *Matter* * to be in effect a Necessary Being, than to be able to remove out of their Minds the Idea of *Immensity,* as Existing Necessarily and inseparably from Eternity. Which Absurdity of

* *Mais peut etre que je raisonne mal,* &c. i e. But perhaps I argue ill when I conclude that the Property my Idea hath to represent Extension, [*that is, in the Sense of the* Cartesians, *Matter*] comes from Extension it self as its Cause; For what hinders me from believing that it theirs

D

this Property comes not from my self, yet at least it may come from some Spirit [*or Being*] Superiour to me, which produces in Me the Idea of Extension, though Extension does not actually exist? theirs, in respect of the Idea of *Immensity*, proves *It* indeed to be Necessary and impossible to be removed. Yet when I consider the thing attentively, I find that my Conclusion is good; and that no Spirit [*or Being*] how excellent soever, can cause the Idea which I have of Extension to represent to me Extension rather than any thing else, if Extension does not actually Exist; because if he should do so, the Idea which I should then have of Extension, would not be a representation of Extension, but a representation of Nothing; which is impossible.

But it may be I still deceive my self, when I say that the Idea I have of Extension, supposes an Object actually existing; For it seems that I have Ideas, which do not suppose any Object; I have, for example the Idea of an Enchanted Castle; though no such thing really Exists. Yet when I consider the difficulty still more attentively; I find there is this difference between the Idea of Extension, and that of an Enchanted Castle; that the first being natural, that is, independent on my Will, supposes an Object which is necessarily such as it represents; whereas the other being artificial, supposes indeed an Object, but it is not necessary that That Object be absolutely such as the Idea represents, because my Will can add to that Object, or diminish from it, as it pleases, as I have before said, and as shall be proved hereafter, when I come to treat of the Origin of Ideas. *Regis Metaphys.* Lib. I. Par. 1. Chap. 3.   ved

ved; but, in respect of *Matter*,
'tis only a perverse applying an
Idea to an Object whereto it
no ways belongs : For, that
it is indeed absolutely impossible and contradictory to suppose Matter necessarily-existing,
shall be demonstrated presently.

2*dly.* From hence it follows, *Nothing*
That *there is no Man whatsoever, so certain*
as the
who makes any use of his Reason, Existence
but may easily become more certain of of a Su-
preme In-
the Being of a Supreme Independent dependent
Cause, than he can be of any Thing Cause.
else besides his own Existence. For
how much Thought soever it may
require to demonstrate the *Other* Attributes of such a Being, as it may do
to demonstrate the greatest Mathematical Certainties; (of which more
hereafter :) Yet as to its *Existence*;
that there *Is* Somewhat Eternal,
Infinite, and Self-existing, which
must be the Cause and Original of
all

all other Things; this is one of
the First and moft natural Conclufions, that any Man, who thinks
at all, can frame in his Mind:
And no Man can any more
doubt of this, than he can doubt
whether twice two be equal to
four. 'Tis poffible indeed a Man
may in fome Senfe be ignorant of
this firft and plain Truth, by being utterly ftupid, and not thinking at all: (For though it is abfolutely impoffible for him to imagine the contrary, yet he may
poffibly neglect to conceive this:
Though no Man can poffibly think
that twice two is not four, yet he
may poffibly be ftupid, and never
have thought at all whether it be
fo or not:) But this I fay; Theie
is no Man, who thinks or reafons
at all, but may eafily become more
certain, that there is Something
Eternal, Infinite, and Self-exifting;

ing ; than he can be certain of any Thing elſe.

3*dly,* Hence we may obſerve, *Of the* That *Our firſt Certainty of the Exi-* *Idea of* *ſtence of God, ariſes not from this,* *God in-* *that in the* Idea *we frame of him in* *cluding* *our own Minds, or rather in the* *Self-ex-* Definition *that we make of the* *iſtence.* Word, [God,] *as ſignifying a Be-* *ing of all poſſible Perfections, we in-* *clude Self-Exiſtence ; but from hence,* *that 'tis demonſtrable both Negative-* *ly, that neither can All Things have* *ariſen out of Nothing, nor can they* *have depended one on another in an* *endleſs Succeſſion, and also poſitive-* *ly, that there is Something in* *the Univerſe,* actually exiſting without us, *the Suppoſition of* *whoſe Non-Exiſtence plainly implies a* *Contradiction.* I do not mean to ſay poſitively, that the Argument drawn from our including Self-Exiſtence in the *Idea* of God, or our comprehending it in the *Definition* or *Notion* we frame of him, is wholly inconclusive and ineffectual to prove his actual Existence. Possibly by a very nice and accurate Deduction, it may be found to be a Satisfactory Proof. But that it is not a Clear and Obvious Demonstration, fitted to convince and put the Atheist to Silence ; appears from the endless Disputes maintained by Learned Men concerning it, without being able to satisfie each other on either side of the Question. The Obscurity and Defect of that Argument, seems to lie in this ; that it extends only to the *Nominal Idea* or *Definition* of a Self-existent Being, and does not with a sufficiently evident Connexion refer and apply that *Nominal Idea, Definition;* or *Notion* which we frame *in our own Mind,* to the **Real Idea** of a

Being

Being *actually existing without us.*
For it is not Satisfactory, that I
have in my Mind an Idea of the
Proposition; *There exists a Being,
indued with all Possible Perfections*;
Or, *There Is a Self-existent Being :*
But I must have also an Idea of *the
Thing.* I must have an Idea of
Something actually existing without
me ; and I must see wherein con-
sists the Absolute Impossibility of
removing that Idea, and consequently of supposing the Non-existence of
the Thing; before I can be satisfi-
ed from that Idea, that the Thing
actually exists. The bare having
an Idea of the Proposition, *There
Is a Self-existent Being,* proves indeed the Thing not to be impossible : (For of an impossible Proposition there is properly no Idea:)
But that it actually Is, cannot be
proved from the Idea ; unless the
Certainty of the Actual Existence of

a Neceſſarily-exiſting Being, follows from the *Poſſibility* of the Exiſtence of ſuch a Being : Which that it does, in this particular Caſe, many Learned Men have indeed thought ; and it is not eaſie to diſprove , becauſe, it muſt be confeſſed, there is ſomething very ſingular in the Idea of Neceſſary Exiſtence : It being evident that if Neceſſary Exiſtence be, (as it undeniably is) a *Poſſible Perfection,* it will conſequently belong *actually* to a Being indued with *All Poſſible Perfections* ; and if it *actually* belongs to ſuch a Being , it will be abſolutely impoſſible that ſuch a Being ſhould *not Exiſt* ; and from hence it ſeems to follow, that it muſt Neceſſarily be true, that ſuch a Being actually Exiſts. This, I ſay, is *not* indeed *eaſie to diſprove.* But it is a *Clearer* and *more Convincing* way of Arguing, to demonſtrate

fijate, that there does actually exist without us a Being, whose Existence is Necessary and of it self ;
from the manifest Contradiction
contained in the contrary Supposition, (as I have before shown ;) and
from the absolute Impossibility of
destroying some Ideas, as of Eternity
and Immensity, which therefore
must needs be the Attributes of a
Necessary Being actually existing.
For if I have an Idea of a Thing, and
cannot possibly in my Imagination
take away the Idea of that Thing
as actually Existing, any more
than I can change or take away the
Idea of the Equality of twice two
to four, the Certainty of the *Ex-*
istence of that Thing, is the same,
and stands on the same Foundation,
as the Certainty of the other *Rela-*
tion : For the Relation of Equality
between twice two and four, has
no other Certainty but this, that I
cannot

cannot, without a Contradiction, change or take away the Idea of that · Relation.   We are *Certain* therefore of the Being of a Supreme Independent Cause; because 'tis strictly demonstrable, that there is Something in the Universe, actually existing without us, the Supposition of whose Non-existence plainly implies a Contradiction.

That the   4thly, From hence it follows, *Material* that *The material World cannot pos-* *World* *cannot* *sibly be the First and Original Being,* *possibly* *Uncreated, Independent, and of* *be the* *Self-Ex-* *it self Eternal.* For since it hath *istent Be-* been already demonstrated, that *ing.* whatever Being hath Existed from Eternity, Independent, and without any External Cause of its Existence ; must be Self-Existent : And that whatever is Self-Existent, must Exist Necessarily, by an Absolute Necessity in the Nature of the Thing it self : It follows evidently,

dently, that unless the Material World Exifts Neceffarily, by an Abfolute Neceffity in its own Nature, fo as that it muft be an Exprefs Contradiction to fuppofe it not to Exift; it cannot be Independent, and of it felf Eternal. Now that the Material World does not Exift thus neceffarily, is very Evident. For Abfolute Neceffity of Exifting, and a Poffibility of not Exifting, being Contradictory Ideas; 'tis manifeft the Material World cannot Exift Neceffarily, if withont a Contradiction we can Conceive it either Not to Be, or to be in any Refpect otherwife than it Now is. Than which Nothing is more eafy. For whether we Confider the *Form* of the World, with the *Difpofition* and *Motion* of its Parts; or whether we confider the *Matter* of it, as fuch, without refpect

to

to its present Form, every Thing in it, both the *Whole* and every one of its *Parts*, their *Situation* and *Motion*, the *Form* and also the *Matter*, are the most Arbitrary and Dependent Things, and the farthest removed from Necessity, that can possibly be imagined.   A Necessity indeed of *Fitneß*, that is, a Necessity that Things should be as they are, in order to the *Well-being* of the whole, there may be in all these Things : But an Absolute Necessity of *Nature* in any of them; (which is what the Atheist must maintain) there is not the least appearance of. If any Man will say in this Sense, (as every Atheist must do,) either that the *Form* of the World, or at least the *Matter* and *Motion* of it, is necessary ; Nothing can possibly be invented more Absurd.

If

If he fays that the particular *Form* The *Form of the World not neceffary.*
is Neceffary ; he muft affirm it to
be a Contradiction to fuppofe that
any Part of the World can be in
any Refpect otherwife than it now
is : It muft be a Contradiction in
Terms, to fuppofe more or fewer
Stars, more or fewer Planets, or to
fuppofe their Size, Figure or Motion, Different from what it now is ;
or to fuppofe more or fewer
Plants and Animals upon Earth,
or the prefent ones of different
Shape and Bignefs from what they
now are : In all which things
there is the greateft Arbitrarinefs,
in refpect of Power and Poffibility, that can be imagined ; however neceffary any of them may
be, in refpect of Wifdom, and
Prefervation of the Beauty and
Order of the whole.

If the Atheift will fay, that the *Nor its Motion.*
Motion in general of all Matter is neceffary :

ceffary: It follows that it muft be a Contradiction in Terms, to fuppofe any matter to be at Reft; Which is fo abfurd and ridiculous, that I think hardly any Atheifts, either Antient or Modern, have prefumed directly to fuppofe it.

* *Mr.*
Toland
Let. III.

One late * Author indeed has ventur'd to affert, and pretended to prove, that *Motion*, that is, the *Conatus to Motion*, is effential to all Matter: But how Philofophically, may appear from this One Confideration. The effential *Conatus to Motion* of every one or of any one Particle of Matter in this Author's imaginary infinite *Plenum*, muft be either a *Conatus* to move fome one determinate way at once, or to move every way at once: A *Conatus* to move fome one determinate way, cannot be effential to any Particle of Matter, but muft arife from fome External Caufe;

Cauſe ; becauſe there is nothing in the pretended Neceſſary Nature of any Particle, to determine its Motion neceſſarily and eſſentially one way rather than another : And a *Conatus* equally to move every way at once, is either an abſolute Contradiction, or at leaſt could produce nothing in Matter but an Eternal Reſt of all and every one of its Parts. But to proceed.

If the Atheiſt will ſuppoſe Motion neceſſary and eſſential to *ſome* Matter, but not to *all :* The ſame Abſurdity as to the Determination of Motion, ſtill follows; and now he moreover ſuppoſes an Abſolute Neceſſity not Univerſal ; that is, that it ſhall be a Contradiction to ſuppoſe ſome certain Matter at Reſt, tho' at the ſame time ſome other Matter actually be ſo.

If he only affirms bare *Mat-* *Nor the* ter to be Neceſſary : Then, *bare* *Matter.*

beſides

besides the extreme Folly of his attributing *Motion* and the *Form* of the World to Chance; (which Opinion I think all Atheists have now given up, and therefore I shall not think my self obliged to take any Notice of it in the Sequel of this Discourse;) it may be demonstrated thus, (out of many the like Arguments that might be drawn from the Nature and Affections of the Thing it self) that bare Matter is not a Necessary Being. If bare Matter be the Necessarily-existing Being, (for that there can be but *One* such, shall be proved hereafter,) then in that Necessary Existence there is either included the Power of Gravitation, or not: If not, then in a World *merely Material*, and in which no *Intelligent Being* presides, there never could have been any Motion; because Motion, as has

been

been already ſhewn, and is now granted in the Queſtion, is not Ne-ceſſary *of it ſelf*: But if the Pow-er of Gravitation *be* included in the Neceſſary Exiſtence of Matter; (which yet is impoſſible, becauſe the Idea of Gravitation is ſeparable fiom that of Matter, and Matter may be conceived without it;) then it is included either in the Neceſſary Exiſtence of All Mat-ter, or of Some only: If of *Some* only, then Matter is not a Similar Being, and con-ſequently not Neceſſary: For in Abſolute Neceſſity, there can be no variety, any more than there can be Degrees. But if Gravita-tion be an Univerſal Quality or Affection of *All Matter*; then there is a Vacuum; (as is abundantly demonſtrated by Mr. *Newton*:) And if there be a Vacuum, then Matter is not a Neceſſary Being;

E   For

For 'tis more than poffible for it, not to Be. If an Atheift will yet Affert, that Matter may be neceffary, though not neceffary to be every where : I anfwer ; this is an exprefs Contradiction : For *abfolute* Neceffity, is abfolute Neceffity every where alike : And if it be no Impoffibility for Matter to be abfent from one Place, 'tis no Impoffibility (abfolutely in the Nature of the Thing ; For no Relative or Confequential Neceffity, can have any Room in this Argument : 'Tis no abfolute Impoffibility, I fay, in the Nature of the Thing,) that Matter fhould be abfent from any other Place, or from every Place.

Spinoza, the moft celebrated Pation of Atheifm in our Time, who taught that * there is no Difference of Subftances ; but that the Whole

Spino-za's Opinion confuted.

* Una fubftantia non poteft produci ab alia fubftantia. *Ethic, P.* I. *Prop.* 6.

Whole and every Part of *the Material World* is a Necessarily-existing Being; and that † there is no other God, but the Universe : That he might seemingly avoid the manifold Absurdities of that Opinion ; endeavours by an Ambiguity of Expression in the Progress of his Discourse, to elude the Arguments by which he foresaw his Assertion would be confuted : For, having at first plainly asserted, that *
All Substance is Necessarily-existing ; he would afterward seem to explain it away, by asserting, that ‖ the Reason why every thing ‖ ex-

Omnis substantia est necessario infinita. *I-bid. Prop.* 8.

Ad naturam substantiæ pertinet existere. *I-bid. Prop.* 7.

† Præter Deum nulla dari neq; concipi potest substantia. *Ibid. Prop.* 14.

* Ad naturam substantiæ pertinet existere. *Prop.* 7.

‖ Res nullo alio modo, neq; alio ordine a Deo produci potuerunt, quam productæ sunt. *Prop.* 33.

Ex Necessitate Divinæ Naturæ, infinita infinitis modis, (hoc est, omnia quæ sub intellectum infinitum cadere possunt) sequi debent. *Prop.* 16

E 2

ists

ists necessarily, and could not possibly have been in any respect different from what it Now is, is because every thing flows from the *Necessity of the Divine Nature.* By which if the unwary Reader understands, that he means things are therefore Necessarily such as they are, because Infinite Wisdom and Goodness could not possibly make Things but in that Order which is Fittest and Wisest in the Whole; he is very much mistaken : For such a Necessity, is not a Natural, but only a Moral and Consequential Necessity ; and directly contrary to the Author's true Intention.   Further, if the Reader hereby understands, that God was determined, not by a Necessity of Wisdom and Goodness, but by a mere Natural Necessity, exclusive of Will and Choice, to make all Things just as they now are ; neither

ther is this the whole of *Spinoza's*
meaning : For this, as abſurd as it
is, is ſtill ſuppoſing God, as a Subſtance diſtinct from the Material
World ; which * He expreſsly de- ˣ *Loc.ſu-*
nies. Nay further, if any one *pra cita-*
thinks his meaning to be, that all *tis.*
Subſtances in the World, are only
Modifications of the Divine Eſſence, neither is This *All :* For thus
God may ſtill be ſuppoſed as an
Agent, acting upon *himſelf* at leaſt,
and manifeſting *himſelf* in different
manners, according to his own Will :
Which † *Spinoza* ex-
preſly denies. But his   † *Deum non operari*
true meaning therefore,   *ex libertate voluntatis.*
however darkly and   *Prop.* 32. *Corol.* 1. &
ambiguouſly he ſome-   *Scholium ad Prop.* 17.
times ſpeaks, muſt be this, and
if he means any thing at all
conſiſtent with himſelf, can
be no other than this : That,

E 3   ſince

since it is absolutely * impossible for any thing to be created or produced by another; and † also absolutely impossible for God to have caused any thing to be in any respect different from what it now is ; every thing that exists, must needs be *so* a || Part of the Divine Substance, not as a Modification caused in it by any * Will or Good-Pleasure or Wisdom in the whole, but as of Absolute Necessity in it self, with respect to the † *manner* of the Existence of each Part, no less than with respect to the Self-Existence of the whole. Thus the Opinion of *Spinoza*, when expressed

* Una substantia non potest produci ab alia substantia *Prop*. 6.

† Res nullo alio modo neq, alio ordine a Deo produci potuerunt, quam productæ sunt. *Prop.* 33.

|| Præter Deum nulla dari, neq; concipi potest substantia. *Prop.* 14.

* Deum non operari ex Libertate voluntatis. *Prop.* 32. *Coroll.* 1.

† Nullo alio *Modo*, neq, *Ordine*, &c.

fed plainly and confiftently, comes evidently to this : That *the Material World,* and every Part of it, with the order and manner of Being of each Part, is the only Self-Exiftent, or Neceffarily-Exifting Being. And now Confequently, he muft of Neceffity affirm all the Conclufions, which I have before fhown to follow demonftrably from that Opinion. He cannot poffibly avoid affirming that 'tis a Contradiction, (not *to the Perfections of God* ; For that is mere fenfelefs Cant and Amufement in Him who maintains that there is but One Subftance in the Univerfe ; But he muft affirm that it is *in it felf and in Terms* a Contradiction,) for any thing to be, or to be imagined, in any refpect otherwife than it Now is. He muft fay 'tis a Contradiction, to fuppofe the *Number,* or *Figure,* or *Order* of the Principal Parts of the World, could

F 4   poffibly

possibly have been different from what they Now are. He must say Motion is neceſſary *of it ſelf*; and consequently that 'tis a Contradicti-ction in Terms, to ſuppoſe any Matter to be at Reſt: Or elſe He muſt affirm, (which is rather the more abſurd of the two, as may appear from what has been already ſaid in proof of the *Second* General Head of the foregoing Diſcourſe: And yet he has * choſen to affirm it;) that Motion, as a Dependent Being, has been eternally communicated from one piece of Matter to another, without having at all any Original Cauſe of its Being, either within it ſelf or from without: Which, with other the like Conſequences, touching the Neceſſity of the Exiſtence of Things; the

+ Corpus motum, vel quieſcens, ad motum vel quietem determinari debuit ab alio corpore, quod etiam ad motum vel quietem determinatum fuit ab alio, & illud iterum ab alio, & ſic in infinitum. *Par.* II. *Prop.* 13. *Lemma* 3.

the very mention of which, is a sufficient Confutation of any Opinion they follow from, do, as I have said, unavoidably follow from the foremention'd Opinion of *Spinoza*: And consequently that Opinion, *viz. That the Universe or Whole World is the Self-existent or Necessarily-existing Being,* is demonstrated to be false.

I have in this Attempt to show, that *The Material World cannot possibly be the First and Original Being, Uncreated, Independent, and Self-existent,* designedly omitted the Argument usually drawn from the supposed absolute Impossibility in the Nature of the Thing it self, of the Worlds being Eternal, or having existed through an Infinite Succession of Time. And this I have done for the two following Reasons.

1*st* Because the Question between us and the Atheists, is not, whether

Of the Opinion concerning the Eternity of the World

whether the *World* can *poſſibly*
have been Eternal ; but *whether it*
can poſſibly be the Original, Inde-
pendent, and Self-Exiſting Being :
which is a very different Queſtion:
For many, who have affirmed the
One, have ſtill utterly denied the
Other : And almoſt all the Antient Philoſophers that held the
Eternity of the World, in whoſe
Authority and Reaſons our Modern Atheiſts do ſo mightily
Boaſt and Triumph ; defended
that their Opinion by ſuch Arguments, as ſhow plainly that they
did by no means thereby intend
to aſſert, that the material World
was the Original, Independent,
Self-Exiſting Being, in Oppoſition to the Belief of the Exiſtence
of a Supreme All-governing *Mind,*
which is the Notion of God.
So that the Deniers of the Being
of God, have no manner of Advantage from that Opinion of the
Eternity

Eternity of the World, even supposing it could not be disproved.
Almost all the old Philosophers,
I say, who held the Eternity of
the World, did not thereby mean
(at least their Arguments do not
tend to prove) that it was Independent and Self-Existent ; but
their Arguments are wholly le-
velled, either to prove barely
that Something must needs · be
Eternal, and that the Universe
could not possibly arise out
of Nothing absolutely and without Cause ; which is all that
Ocellus Lucanus's Arguments a-
mount to : Or else that the
World is an Eternal and Necessary Effect, flowing from the Essent-
tial and Immutable Energy of the
Divine Nature ; which seems to
have been *Aristotle's* Opinion : Or
else that the World is an Eternal Voluntary Emanation from
the All-Wise and Supreme Cause ;
which

which was the Opinion of many of *Plato's Followers*. None of which Opinions or Arguments, will in the least help out our modern Atheists; who would exclude Supreme *Mind* and Intelligence out of the Universe. For however the Opinion of the Eternity of the World, is really inconsistent with the Belief of its being Created in time: yet so long as the Defenders of that Opinion, either did not think it Inconsistent with the Belief of the World's being the Effect and Work of an E-ternal, All-Wise and All-Powerful Mind; or at least could defend that Opinion by such Arguments only, as did not in the least prove the Self-Existence or Independency of the World, but most of them rather quite the contrary, 'Tis with the greatest Injustice and Unreasonableness in the World, that our Modern Atheists

(to

(to whose Purpose the Eternity or Non-Eternity of the World would signifie nothing, unless at the same Time the Existence and Sovereignty of Eternal Intelligence or Mind were likewise disproved,) pretend either the Authority or the Reasons of these Men to be on their side.

Ocellus Lucanus, one of the ancientest Asserters of the Eternity of the World; whose Antiquity and Authority * Mr. *Blount* opposes to that of *Moses*, in delivering his Opinion, speaks indeed like one that believed the Material World to be Self-existent; asserting, † that *it is utterly incapable either*

ᵞ *Oracles of Reason; Letter to Mr Gildon,* p. 216.

† Ἀγένητον τὸ πᾶν κỳ ἀνώλεθρον.

Ἄναρχον κỳ ἀτελδ τητην. Κόσμ⊙ αὐτὸς ἐξ ἑαυτῦ αἰδιός ἐςι κỳ αὐτοπλὴς κỳ διαμένων ᾗ πάντα αἰῶνα.

Ἀ̇ε ὄντ⊙ τῦ κόπυ, ἀναγχαῖον κỳ τὰ μέρη αὐτῦ ζωντάρχοι. Λέγω ᾗ μέρη, ἐρανὸν, γῆν, &c. *Ocellus Lucan.* Περὶ ᾗ τῦ παντὸς φύσεως.

of Generation or Corruption, of Be-
ginning or End; that *it is of it*
self Eternal and Perfect and Perma-
nent for ever; and that *the Frame*
and Parts of the World must needs
be Eternal, as well as the Substance
and Matter of the Whole : But when
he comes to produce his Arguments or Reasons for his Opinion;
they are either so very absurd and
ridiculous, that even any *Atheist*
in this Age ought to be ashamed
to repeat them; as when he
proves * that *the World*
must needs be Eternal,
without Beginning or
End, because both its
Figure and Motion are a

* Τὸ ἄναρχον ἐ ἀτελεύτη-
τον τῆς γή ταῖσ ἐ τ κινήσεως,
πιςῦ ἡ διότι ἀγένητ ὁ κοσ-
μ ἐ ἄφθαρτ. ἦτε γ τὸ
γήματ ἴ ἵνα, κύκλ ἐ
ἢ πάντοθεν ἴσ ἐ ὅμοι,
λόγ ἄναρχ ἐ ἀτελεύτη-
τ. ἦτε τ κινήσεως&c. I-
bid.

Thus *Translated* : Nay that the Figure, Motion, &c.
thereof, are without Beginning and End; thereby it
plainly appears, that the World admitteth neither
Production nor Dissolution · For the Figure is Spheri-
cal, and consequently on every side equal, and therefore without Beginning or Ending. Also the motion
is circular, &c. *Oracles of Reason* p. 215.

Circle

Circle, which has neither Beginning nor End : Or elſe they are ſuch Arguments as prove only what no Man ever really denied ; *viz.* That Something muſt be Eternal, becauſe 'tis impoſſible for Every Thing to ariſe out of Nothing, or to fall into Nothing ; As when he ſays † that *the World muſt have been Eternal, becauſe 'tis a Contradi-Ction for the Univerſe to have had a Begin-ning ; ſince if it had a Beginning, it muſt have been cauſed by Some-thing, and then it is not the Uni-verſe.* To which One Argument, all that he ſays in his whole Book, is plainly reducible. So that 'tis evident, all that he really proves, is only this , that there muſt needs be an Eternal Being in the Univerſe : and not, that Matter is Self-exiſtent, in Oppoſition to

Intel-

† Ἀγένητον τὸ πᾶν ——— ἐξ ὁ γὰρ γέγονεν, ἐκ τῖνο ϖρῶ-τον τῦ παντός ὅςιν ——— Τόγε ἢ πᾶν γινόμβρον, σιω πᾶσι γί-νεϑ· ἡ τῦτο γὰ ἡ ἀδύνατον—— Ἐκτὸς γὰ τῦ Παντὶς ὁδὲν Ocell. ibid.

Intelligence and Mind. For, all that he asserts about the absolute Necessity of the *Order and Parts* of the World, is confessedly most ridiculous, not at all proved by the Arguments he alleges : And in some Passages of this very Book, as well as in other Fragments, He himself supposes, and is forced expresly to confess, that, however Eternal and Necessary every thing in the World be imagined to be, yet even That Necessity must flow from an + *Eternal and Intelligent Mind,* the Necessary Perfections of whose Nature are the Cause † *of the Harmony and Beauty of the World,* and particularly of Mens having ‖ *Faculties, Organs of Sense, Appetites,* &c. fitted even to *Final Causes.*

* Τὸ ἀνκίσηπν, θειον ιμὸ, καὶ λόγον ἔχον ἐμφρον Gicll. *Luc. de Leg. fragm.*

† Συνέχει ἢ κόσμον ἁρμοτία, Ταύτης δ' αἰτιθ ὁ Εἰ ός. *Ibid*

‖ Τὰς δυνάμεις, καὶ τὰ Οργανα, καὶ τὰς ὀρέξεις ὑπὸ Θεῖ δεδομένας αι ϑρώποις, ἐχ ἡδονῆς ἕνεκα δεδόσθαι συμβέβηκεν, ἀλλὰ, &c. *Idem* Περὶ ὁ τῶ πανπε φύσεως.

Ariſtotle likewiſe, was a great Aſſerter indeed of the Eternity of the World : But not in Oppoſition to the Belief of the Being, or of the Power, Wiſdom, or Goodneſs of God : On the contrary He for no other Reaſon aſſerted the World to be Eternal, but becauſe he fancied that ſuch an Effect muſt needs eternally proceed from ſuch an eternal Cauſe. And ſo far was he from teaching, that Matter is the Firſt and Original Cauſe of all Things ; that on the contrary he every where expreſly deſcribes God to be an * *Intelligent Being*, † *In-* corporeal, ‖ *The Firſt Mover of all Things, Himſelf Immoveable* ; and affirms, that * *if there were nothing but Matter in the World, there would be no Original Cauſe, but an Infinite*

* Νȣ̃;
† Θεòν ἀσώμα τον ἐπίπνρε *Diog. in vi-ta Ariſtot*
‖ Τò πρῶ- τον κινȣν, ἀκίνητον *Ariſtot Metaph.*

× Εἰ μὴ ἔςαι περὰ τὰ ται τὰ ἄλλα, ȣκ ἔςαι ἀρχὴ ᾗ τάξις, ἀλ' ἀϊ ἀ ἀρχῆς ἀρχὴ *Ibid.*

F   Pro-

Progreſſion of Cauſes, which is abſurd.

. As to thoſe Philoſophers, who taught plainly and expreſly, that Matter was not only Eternal, but alſo Self-exiſtent and entirely Independent, Co-exiſting from Eternity with God, independently as a Second Principle : I have already ſhown the Impoſſibility of this Opinion, at the Entrance upon the preſent Head of Diſcourſe, where I proved that Matter could not poſſibly be *Self-exiſtent :* And I ſhall further demonſtrate it to be Falſe, when I come to prove the *Unity* of the Self-exiſtent Being.

Plato, whatever his Opinion was about the Original Matter, very largely and fully declares his Sentiments about the Formation of the World, *viz.* that it was compoſed and framed by an Intelligent and

and Wise God; and there is no One of all the Antient Philosophers, who in all his Writings speaks so excellently and worthily * as He, concerning the Nature and Attributes of God. Yet as to the Time of the World's Beginning to be Formed, He seems to make it indefinite, when he says, † *The World must needs be an Eternal Resemblance of the Eternal Idea.* At least his Followers afterward so understood and explained it, as if by the Creation of the World, was not to be understood a Creation

* ὁ ποιητής καὶ πατήρ τοῦδε τοῦ παντός

ὁ γῆν, ἐργνὸν καὶ Θεὸς, καὶ πάντα τὰ ἐν ἐργνῷ καὶ τὰ ἐν ᾅδε, καὶ ὑπὸ γῆς ἅπαντα ἐργασάμεν·. *De Republ. Lib.* 10.

† Πᾶσα ἀνάγκη τόνδε κόσμον, εἰκόνα τινὸς ἐῖ. *Plato in Timæo.* *Which Words being very imperfect in our Copies of the Original, are thus rendered by* Cicero. *Si ergo generatus* [est mundus,] *ad id effectus est, quod ratione sapientiaq; comprehenditur, atq; immutabili æternitate continetur. Ex quo efficitur, ut sit necesse hunc, quem cernimus, mundum, simulachrum æternum esse alicujus æterni* Cic. de Univers.

in Time; * but only in Order of Nature, Causality and Dependence: That is; that the Will of God, and his Power of Acting, being necessarily as Eternal as his Essence, † the Effects of that Will and Power might

* Qui autem a Deo quidem factum fatentur, non tamen eum volunt *Temporis* habere, sed suæ *Creationis* initium; ut modo quodam vix intelligibili, Semper sit factus. *Augustin. de Civit. Dei. Lib.* 11. *Cap.* 4.

De Mundo, & de his quos in mundo deos a Deo factos scribit Plato, apertissime dicit eos esse cæpisse, & habere initium.------Verum id quomodo intelligant, invenerunt [Platonici;] non esse hoc videlicet *Temporis,* sed *Substitutionis* initium. *Ibid. Lib.* 10. *Cap.* 31.

Sed mundum quidem fuisse semper, Philosophia auctor est, conditore quidem Deo, sed non ex tempore *Macrob. in Somn. Scip. Lib.* 2. *Cap.* 10.

† Καὶ οἱ Βέλη, παραδείγματι σοι περὶ τῶν γνωρίμων, ἐξετάζειν πρὸς τὸ ζητούμενον. φασὶ γὰρ ὅτι καθάπερ αἴτιον τὸ σῶμα τῆς ἑαυτῆ σκιᾶς γίνεται ὁμόχρονΘ ᾗ τῷ σώματι ἡ σκιὰ καὶ οὐχ ὁμότιμΘ ἔτω δὴ καὶ ὅδε ὁ κόσμΘ προσβολὲ ἐνία ὅτι τῷ Θεῦ ἀπ' ἀυτῷ τῦ εἰ), καὶ ζωμιδίος ὅτι τῷ Θεῷ ἐκεῖ δὴ καὶ ὁμότιμΘ *Zacharia Scholast Disputat.*

Sicut enim, inquiunt [Platonici,] si Pes ex æternitate semper fuisset in pulvere, semper ei subesset vestigium, quod tamen vestigium a calcante factum nemo dubitaret, nec alterum altero prius esset, quamvis alterum ab altero factum esset · Sic, inquiunt, & mundus atq; in illo Dii creati, & semper fuerunt; semper existente qui fecit; & tamen facti sunt. *Augustin de Civitate Dei. Lib.* 10. *Cap.* 21

be

be fuppofed coæval to the Will and Power themfelves; in the fame manner, as *Light* would e_ternally proceed from the *Sun*, or a *Shadow* from the *interpofed Body*, or an *Impreffion* from an *impofed Seal*, if the refpective Caufes of thefe Effects were fuppofed Eter_nal.

From all which, it plainly ap_pears how little Reafon our Mo_dern Atheifts have to boaft either of the Authority or Reafons of thofe Antient Philofophers, who held the Eternity of the World. For fince thefe Men neither pro_ved, nor attempted to prove, that the Material World was Original o it felf, Independent, or Self-ex_fting; but only that it was an Eternal Effect of an Eternal Caufe; which is God; 'tis evident that his their Opinion, even fuppo_ing it could by no means be refu_

ted,

ted, could afford no manner of Advantage to the Cause of those Atheists in our days, who excluding Supreme Mind and Intelligence out of the Universe, would fain make mere Matter and Necessity the Original and Eternal Cause of all Things.

2*dly.* The other Reason, why in this Attempt to Prove that *the Material World cannot possibly be the First and Original Being, Uncreated, Independent and Self-Existent;* I have omitted the Argument usually drawn from the supposed absolute Impossibility of the Worlds being Eternal, or having Existed through an Infinite Succession of Time; is *because that Argument,* however true it may be in it self, *can never be so stated, as to be of any use in Convincing or Affecting the Mind of an Atheist,* who must not be supposed to come prepared beforehand

forehand with any tranfcendent
Idea of the Eternity of God.
For Since an Atheift cannot be
fuppofed to Believe the Nice and
Subtle Diftinctions of the Schools;
'tis impoffible by this Argument
fo to difprove the Poffibility of the
Eternity of the World, but that
an Atheift will underftand it to
prove equally againft the Poffibility of any thing's being Eternal,
and confequently that it proves
nothing at all, but is only a Difficulty arifing from our not being
able to comprehend adequately
the Notion of Eternity. That the
Material World is not Self-Exiftent or Neceffarily-Exifting, but
the Product of an Intelligent and
Wife Agent, may (as I have already fhown) be ftrictly demonftrated by bare Reafon againft the
moft Obftinate Atheift in the
World: But the *Time When* the
World

World was Created, or whether
its Creation was, *properly speaking,*
in Time; is not so easy to demonstrate strictly by bare Reason, (as
appears from the Opinions of
many of the Antient Philosophers concerning that matter,)
but the Proof of it ought to
be taken from Revelation. To
indeavour to prove, that there
cannot possibly be any such thing as
infinite Time or *Space*, from the Impossibility of an * Addition of
Finite Parts ever composing or ex-
hausting an Infinite : or from the
imaginary *inequality of the Num-*
ber of Years, Days, and Hours
that would be contained in the
one ; or of the Miles, Yards, and
Feet, that would be contained
in the other; is supposing Infinites
to be made up of *Numbers* of
Finites, that is, 'tis supposing
Finite Quantities to be *Aliquot* or
Con-

'Cud-
worth
System p.
643.

Conſtituent Parts of Infinite ; when indeed they are not ſo, but do all *Equally*, whether *Great* or *Small*, whether *Many* or *Few*, bear the very ſame proportion to an Infinite, as Mathematical Points do to a Line, or Lines to a Superficies, or as Moments do to Time ; that is, None at all. So that to argue abſolutely againſt the Poſſibility of Infinite Space or Time, merely from the imaginary inequality of the *Numbers* of their Finite Parts ; which are not properly Conſtituent Parts, but mere Nothings in Proportion, is the very ſame thing as it would be to argue againſt the Poſſibility of the Exiſtence of any determinate Finite Quantity, from the imaginary Equality or Inequality of the *Number* of the Mathematical Lines and Points contained therein ; when indeed neither the one nor the other has (in

propriety

propriety of Speech) any *Num-ber* at all, but they are abſolutely *without Number* : Neither can any Number or Quantity be any *Ali-quot* or *Conſtituent* Part of Infinite, or be compared at all with it, or bear any kind of Proportion to it, or be the Foundation of any Ar-gument in any Queſtion concern-ing it.

The Eſ-ſence of the Self-exiſtent Being In-compre-henſible.　IV. *What the Subſtance or Eſ-ſence of that Being, which is Self-Exiſtent, or Neceſſarily-Exiſting, is; we have no Idea, neither is it poſ-ſible for us in any meaſure to com-prehend it.* That there is ſuch a Being, actually Exiſting without us, we are ſure (as I have already ſhown) by ſtrict and undeniable Demonſtration. Alſo what it is *not* ; that is, that the Material World is *not* it, as our Modern Atheiſts

Atheiſts would have it; has been already Demonſtrated. But what it *is,* I mean as to its Subſtance and Eſſence; this we are infinitely unable to comprehend. Yet does not this in the leaſt Diminiſh the Certainty of the Demonſtration of its Exiſtence. For it is one Thing, to know certainly that a Being Exiſts; and another, to know what the Eſſence of that Being is: And the one may be capable of the ſtricteſt Demonſtration, when the other is abſolutely beyond the Reach of all our Faculties to underſtand. A Blind or Deaf Man has infinitely more Reaſon to deny the Being, or the Poſſibility of the Being, of Light or Sounds; than any Atheiſt can have to deny, or doubt of, the Exiſtence of God. For the one can at the utmoſt have no other Proof, but credible Teſtimony

mony, of the Existence of certain Things, whereof it is absolutely impossible that he himself should frame any manner of Idea, not only of their Essence, but even of their Effects or Properties ; But the Other may with the least use of his Reason be assured of the Existence of a Supreme Being by undeniable Demonstration , and may also certainly know abundance of its Attributes, (as shall be made appear in the following Propositions,) though its Essence be intirely incomprehensible. Wherefore nothing can be more Unreasonable and Weak, than for an Atheist upon this account to deny the Being of God, merely because his weak and finite Understanding cannot Frame to it self any Notion of the Substance or Essence of that First and Supreme Cause. We are utterly ignorant

of

of the Suſtance or Eſſence of all
other things ; even of thoſe things
which we converſe moſt familiarly
with, and think we underſtand
beſt. There is not ſo contemptible
a Plant or Animal, that does not
confound the moſt inlarged Underſtanding upon Earth : Nay even
the ſimpleſt and plaineſt of all inanimate Beings, have their Eſſence
or Subſtance hidden from Us in the
deepeſt and moſt impenetrable Ob-
ſcurity. How weak then and fooliſh is it to raiſe Objections againſt
the Being of God, from the In-
comprehenſibleneſs of his Eſſence !
and to repreſent it as a ſtrange
and incredible thing, that there
ſhould Exiſt any Incorporeal Subſtance, the Eſſence of which we
are not able to Comprehend ! As
if it were not far more ſtrange,
that there ſhould exiſt numberleſs Objects of our Senſes, Things
ſub-

subject to our daily Inquiry, Search and Examination ; and yet we not be able, no not in any measure, to find out the real Essence of any one even of the least of *these* Things.

From what has been said upon this Head, we may observe,

Of Infinite Space. 1*st* *The Weakness of Such,* as *have presumed to imagin Infinite Space to be a just Representation or adæquate Idea of the Essence of the Supreme Cause.* This is a weak and fond Imagination, arising from hence, that Men using themselves to Judge of all Things by their Senses only, fancy Spiritual or Immaterial Substances, because they are not Objects of their Corporeal Senses, to be mere Nothings ; Just as Children imagin Air, because they cannot see it, to be mere Emptiness and Nothing. But the Fallacy is too gross, to deserve being

being Infifted upon. There are Numberlefs Subftances in the World, whofe Effences are as intirely unknown and impoffible to be reprefented to our Imaginations, as Colours are to a Man that was Born Blind, or Sounds to One that has been always Deaf: Nay, there is no Subftance in the World, of which we know any thing further, than only a certain Number of its Properties or Attributes; of which we know fewer in fome things, and in Others more. Infinite Space, is nothing elfe but an abftract Idea of Immenfity or Infinity; even as Infinite Duration, is of Eternity: And it would be not much lefs proper, to fay that Eternity is the Effence of the Supreme Caufe, than to fay, that Immenfity is fo. Indeed they feem Both to be but Attributes of an Effence Incomprehenfible to Us;

and

and when we indeavour to repreſent the real Subſtance of any Being whatſoever in our weak imaginations, we ſhall find ~~our~~ ſelves in like manner deceived.

The Va-
nity of the
School-
men.

2*dly.* From hence appears the *Vanity of the Schoolmen,* who as in other Matters, ſo in their Diſputes about the Self-Exiſtent Being ; when they come at what they are by no means able to comprehend or explain ; leaſt they ſhould ſeem ignorant of any thing, they give us Terms of Art, and Words of Amuſement ; which under pretence of explaining the matter before them, ſeem really to have no manner of Idea or Signification at all. Thus, when they tell us concerning the Eſſence of God, that He is *Purus Actus, mera forma,* and the like ; either the Words have no Meaning, and ſignifie nothing ; or elſe they

they expreſs only the Perfection of his *Power*, and other Attributes, which is not what theſe Men intend to expreſs by them.

V. Though the Subſtance or Eſſence of the Self-Exiſtent Being, is it ſelf abſolutely Incomprehenſible to us : yet many of the Eſſential Attributes of his Nature are ſtrictly Demonſtrable, as well as his Exiſtence. Thus in the firſt place the Self-Exiſtent Being muſt of neceſſity be Eternal. The Idea's of Eternity and Self-Exiſtence are ſo cloſely connected, that becauſe Something muſt of Neceſſity be Eternal *Independently and without any outward Cauſe of its Being*, therefore it muſt neceſſarily be Self-exiſtent ; and becauſe it is impoſſible but Something muſt be Self-exiſtent, therefore it is neceſſary that it muſt likewiſe be

That the Self-Exiſtent Being muſt be Eternal.

G

Eter-

Eternal. To be Self-exiſtent is (as has been already ſhown) to Exiſt by an Abſolute Neceſſity in the Nature of the Thing it ſelf. Now this Neceſſity being Abſolute, and not depending upon any thing External, muſt be always unalterably the ſame; Nothing being alterable, but what is capable of being affected by Something without it ſelf. That Being therefore, which has no other Cauſe of its Exiſtence, but the abſolute Neceſſity of its own Nature; muſt of Neceſſity have exiſted from everlaſting, without Beginning; and muſt of Neceſſity exiſt to everlaſting, without End.

Of the Manner of our Conceiving the Eternity of God. As to the *Manner* of this Eternal Exiſtence, 'tis manifeſt it herein infinitely tranſcends the Manner of the Exiſtence of all Created Beings; even of ſuch as ſhall exiſt for ever, that whereas it is not poſſible for their finite Minds to comprehend

comprehend all that is paſt, or to underſtand perfectly all things that are at preſent, much leſs to know all that is future, or to have entirely in their Power any thing that is to come ; but their Thoughts, and Knowledge and Power, muſt of Neceſſity have degrees and periods, and be ſucceſſive and tranſient as the Things Themſelves : The Eternal, Supreme Cauſe, on the contrary, (ſuppoſing him to be an *Intelligent Being,* which will hereafter be proved in the Sequel of this Diſcourſe,) muſt of Neceſſity have ſuch a perfect, independent and unchangeable Comprehenſion of all things , that there can be no One Point or Inſtant of his Eternal Duration, wherein all Things that are paſt, preſent, or to come, will not be as entirely known and repreſented to him in one ſingle

Thought

Thought or View ; and all Things present and future, be equally intirely in his Power and Direction , as if there was really no Succeffion at all, but all Things were actually prefent at once. Thus far we can fpeak Intelligibly concerning the Eternal Duration of the Self-Exiftent Being; and no *Atheift* can fay that this is an Impoffible, Abfurd or Infufficient Account : It is, in the moft proper and intelligible Senfe of the Words, to all the purpofes of Excellency and Perfection, *Interminabilis vitæ tota fimul & perfecta Poffeffio* : The *entire and perfect Poffeffion of an endlefs Life.*

With respect to Succeffion.   Others have fuppofed that the Difference between the Manner of the Eternal Exiftence of the Supreme Caufe, and that of the Exiftence of Created Beings, is this : That whereas the latter is a continual tranfient Succeffion of Duration ;

tion; the former is one Point or Inſtant comprehending Eternity, and wherein all things are really co-exiſtent. But this Diſtinction I ſhall not now inſiſt upon; as being of no uſe in the preſent Diſpute; becauſe, ſuppoſing it never ſo true, yet it would be hard to prove and explain it in ſuch a manner, as ever to convince an Atheiſt that there is any thing in it: And beſides, as on the one hand the Schoolmen have indeed generally choſen to defend it; ſo on the other hand, there * are many Learned Men of not leſs Underſtanding and Judgment than they;

* Crucem ingenio figere, ut rem capiat fugientem Captum. —— Tam fieri non poteſt, ut inſtans [*Temporis*] coexiſtat rei ſucceſſivæ, quam impoſſibile eſt punctum coexiſtere [*coextendi*] lineæ. —— Luſus merus non intellectorum verborum. *Gaſſend. Phyſic. lib.* 1.

I ſhall not trouble you with the inconſiſtent and unintelligible Notions of the Schoolmen; that it [*the Eternity of God*] is *duratio tota ſimul*, in which we are not to conceive any Succeſſion, but to imagine it in an Inſtant. We may as well conceive the

G 3   who

Immensity of God to be who have rejected and *a Point*, as his *Eternity* opposed it. to be an *Instant.——*

And how that can be together, which must necessarily be imagined to be co-existent to Successions, let them that can, Conceive. *Archbishop Tillotson*, Vol. 7. Serm. 13.

Others say, God sees and knows future things, by the presentiality and co-existence of all things in Eternity, for they say that future things are actually present and existing to God, tho' not *in mensura propria*, yet *in mensura aliena*. The School-Men have much more of this Jargon and canting Language; and I envy no Man the understanding these Phrases, but to me they seem to signifie nothing, but to have been Words invented by idle and conceited Men, which a great many ever since, left they should seem to be ignorant, would seem to understand But I wonder most, that Men, when they have amused and puzled themselves and others with hard Words, should call this *Explaining* Things. *Archbishop Tillotson*, Vol. 6. Serm. 6.

That the Self-Ex-istent Be-ing must be Infi-nite and Omnipre-sent. **VI.** *The Self-Existent Being,* must of Necessity be Infinite and Omni-present. The Idea of Infinity, as well as of Eternity, is so closely connected with that of Self-Existence, that because it is impossible but Something must be Infinite *indepen-dently*

dently and of it self, (for elfe it would be impoffible there fhould be any Infinite at all, unlefs an Effect could be perfecter than its Caufe;) therefore it muft of Neceffity be Self-exiftent; and becaufe Something muft of Neceffity be Self-Exiftent, therefore it is necef-fary that it muft likewife be Infi-nite. To be Self-Exiftent (as has been already fhown,) is to Exift by an Abfolute Neceffity in the Nature of the Thing it felf: Now this Neceffity being Abfo-lute in it felf, and not depending on any Outward Caufe; 'tis evident it muft be *every where*, as well as *always*, unalterably the fame : For a Neceffity which is not every where the fame, is plainly a Con-fequential Neceffity only, depen-ding upon fome External Caufe, and not an Abfolute one in its own Nature : For a Neceffity abfolute-

ly

ly such in it self, has no Relation to Time or Place, or any thing else : Whatever therefore Exists by an Absolute Necessity in its own Nature, must needs be Infinite as well as Eternal. To suppose a Finite Being, Self-Existent, is to say that it is a Contradiction for that Being not to Exist, the Absence of which may yet be conceived without a Contradiction : which is the greatest Absurdity in the World : For if a Being can without a Contradiction be absent from One Place, it may without a Contradiction be absent likewise from another Place, and from all Places : And whatever Necessity it may have of Existing, must arise from some External Cause, and not absolutely from it self ; and consequently the Being, cannot be Self-Existent.

From

From hence it follows,

1*st*. That the Infinity of the Self-Existent Being, must be an Infinity of *Fulness* as well as of *Immensity*, that is, it must not only be without *Limits*, but also without *Diversity*, *Defect*, or *Interruption*. For Instance : Could matter be supposed *Boundless*, it would not therefore follow that it was in this compleat Sense *Infinite* ; because though it had no Limits, yet it might have within it self any assignable Vacuities. But now whatever is Self-Existent, must of Necessity Exist absolutely in every Place alike, and be equally present every where ; and consequently must have a true and absolute Infinity, both of *Immensity* and *Fulness*.

2*dly*. From hence it follows, that the Self-Existent Being, must be a *most Simple, Unchangeable,*

In.

Incorruptible Being, *without Parts,
Figure, Motion, Divisibility,* or
any other such Properties as
we find in Matter. For all
these things do plainly and necessarily imply Finiteness in their
very Notion, and are utterly inconsistent with complete Infinity.
Divisibility is a separation of
Parts, real or mental; (meaning
by mental Separation, not barely
a *partial Apprehending,* but a removing, disjoining, or separating
Parts one from another in the Imagination;) and any such Separation or Removing of Parts, is *really*
or *mentally* a setting Bounds;
either of which, destroys Infinity.
Motion for the same reason implies Finiteness : And *to have
Parts,* properly speaking, signifies
either Difference and Diversity of
Existence , which is inconsistent
with Necessity ; or else it signifies
Divi-

Diviſibility, real or mental as be-
foɪe, which is inconſiſtent with
complete Infinity. *Corruption*,
Change, or any Alteration whatſoever,
implies Motion, Separation of
Parts, and Finiteneſs: And any
manner of *Compoſition*, in oppoſition to the moſt perfeᴄt *Simplicity*,
ſignifies Difference and Diverſity
in the manner of Exiſtence; which
is inconſiſtent with Neceſſity.

'Tis evident therefore, that the
Self-Exiſtent Being muſt be Infinite in the *ſtriᴄteſt* and moſt *complete*
Senſe. But now as to the particular *Manner* of his being Infinite or
every where preſent, in oppoſition
to the manner of Created Things
being preſent in ſuch or ſuch finite places: It is as impoſſible for
our finite Underſtandings, to comprehend or explain; as it is for
us to form an adæquate Idea of
Infinity : Yet that the thing is
true,

Of the Manner of our Conccei-ving the Immenſi-ty of God.

true, that he is actually Omnipre-
sent, we are as certain as we are
that there must Something be Infinite; which no Man who has
thought upon these things at all,
ever denied. The Schoolmen indeed have presumed to assert, that
the Immensity of God is a Point,
as his Eternity is an Instant. But
this being altogether Unintelligible; That which we can more
safely affirm, and which no Atheist can say is absurd, and which
nevertheless is sufficient to all wise
and good Purposes, is this: That
whereas all Finite and Created Beings, can be present but in One
definite Place at Once; and Corporeal Beings even in that One
place very imperfectly and unequal-
ly, to any Purpose of Power or
Activity, only by the Successive
Motion of different Members and
Organs: The Supreme Cause on
the

the contrary, being an Infinite and moſt Simple Eſſence, and comprehending all things perfect-ly in himſelf, is *at all times equal-ly* preſent, both in his Simple Eſſence, and by the Immediate and Perfect Exerciſe of all his Attri-butes, *to every Point* of the Bound-leſs Immenſity, as if it were really all but one Single Point.

VII. *The Self-Exiſtent Being, muſt of Neceſſity be but One.* This evidently follows from his being *Neceſſarily-Exiſtent.* For Neceſſity Abſolute in it ſelf, is Simple and Uniform, without any poſſible Difference or Variety: And all Variety or Difference of Exiſtence, muſt needs ariſe from ſome Exter-nal Cauſe, and be *dependent* upon it. For to ſuppoſe *two* (or more) *different* Natures exiſting *of them-ſelves*

That the Self-Ex-iſtent Be-ing can be but One.

selves, neceffarily, and *independent* from each other; implies this plain *Contradiction;* that each of them being independent from the other, they may either of them be fuppofed to exift alone, fo that it will be no contradiction to imagine the other not to exift, and confequently neither of them will be Neceffarily-Exifting. Whatfoever therefore exifts neceffarily, is the One Simple Effence of the Self-Exiftent Being : and whatfoever differs from that, is not Neceffarily-Exifting : Becaufe in abfolute Neceffity there can be no Difference or Diverfity of Exiftence. Other Beings there may be innumerable, befides the One Infinite Self-Exiftent : But no Other Nature can be Self-Exiftent, becaufe fo it would be individually the fame, at the fame time that it is fuppofed to be different.

From

From hence it follows,

1*st*. That the *Unity* of God, is *Of the Trinity.* an *Unity of Nature* or *Essence* : For of *This* it is that we must be understood, if we would argue Intelligibly, when we speak of Necessity or Self-Existence. As to the *Diversity of Persons* in that One and the same Nature : That is ; whether in the Unity of the Divine Nature, there may not co-exist with the First Supreme Cause, such Emanations from it, as may themselves be equally Eternal, Infinite, and Perfect, by an absolute and complete Communication of all the Divine Attributes in an infinite and perfect degree, excepting only that of Self-Origination : Of this, I say ; as there is nothing in bare Reason, by which it can be demonstrated that there is actually any such thing ; so neither is there any

Argument,

Argument, by which it can be proved impossible or unreasonable to be supposed, and therefore when declared and made known to us by clear Revelation, it ought to be believed.

The Impossibility of two Independent Principles. 2*dly.* From hence it follows, That *it is impossible there should be two different Self-existent Independent Principles, as some Philosophers have imagined, such as God and Matter.* For since Self-Existence is Necessary Existence; and since it is an express Contradiction (as has already been shown) that two different Natures should each be Necessarily-existing, it evidently follows, that 'tis absolutely impossible there should be Two Independent Self-existent Principles, such as *God and Matter.*

The Error of Spinoza. 3*dly.* From hence we may observe the Vanity, Folly and Weakness of *Spinoza :* who because Self-exi-

stent

ſtent Nature muſt neceſſarily be but One, concludes from thence, that *the whole World, and every thing contained therein, is One Uniform Subſtance, Eternal, Uncreated and Neceſſary :* Whereas juſt on the contrary he ought to have concluded, that becauſe all things in the World are very different one from another, and have all manner of Variety and all the Marks of Will and Arbitrarineſs and Changeableneſs, (and none of Neceſſity) in them, being plainly fitted with very different Powers to very different Ends, and diſtinguiſhed one from another by a diverſity; not only of Modes, but alſo of eſſential Attributes, and conſequently (if we have any Knowledge at all of

Unà ſubſtantia non poteſt produci ab alia. *Ethic. Par. I. Prop. 6.*

Ad naturam ſubſtantiæ pertinet exiſtere. *Prop.* 7.

Præter Deùm nullà dari, neq, concipi poteſt ſubſtantia. *Prop.* 14.

H   them)

them) of their Subftances themfelves alfo ; therefore *none of thefe
things are neceffary or Self-exiftent,
but muft needs depend all upon fome
External Caufe, that is, on the One Supreme, Unchangeable, Self-exiftent Being.* That which led *Spinoza* into his
foolifh and deftructive Opinion, and
on which alone all his *Argumentation*
is entirely built, is that *abfurd* Definition of Subftance ;

† Per fubftantiam In-
telligo id, quod in fe
eft, & per fe concipi-
tur ; hoc eft, id cujus
conceptus non indiget
conceptu alterius rei,
a quo formari debeat.
Definitio 3. *Which pre-
fently after he thus ex-
plains* Ad naturam
fubftantiæ pertinet Ex-
iftere, hoc eft, ipfius
effentia involvit necef-
fario exiftentiam. *E-
thic. Par.* I. *Prop.* 7.

† that *it is Something,
the Idea of which does
not depend on, or pre-
fuppofe, the Idea of any
other thing, from which
it might proceed ; but
includes in it felf Ne-
ceffary-exiftence.* Which
Definition is either
falfe and fignifies no-
thing ; and then his
whole Doctrine built upon it,
falls at once to the Ground : Or
if

if it be true ; then neither Matter, nor Spirit, nor any *Finite* Being whatsoever, (as has been before shown) is in that Sense properly a Substance, but (*the* ὁ ὤν) the Self-existent Being alone ; and so it will prove Nothing (notwithstanding all his *Show* and *Form* of Demonstration,) to his main Purpose ; which was, to make us believe that there is no such Thing as Power or Liberty in the Universe, but that * every particular thing in the World is by an Absolute Necessity just what it is, and could not possibly have been in any respect otherwise : Supposing, I say, his Definition of Substance to be true ; yet even *That* would really conclude nothing to his main Purpose concerning the Necessity of all Things : For since,

* Res nullo alio modo, neq; alio ordine, a Deo produci potuerunt, quam productæ funt. *Prop.* 33.

H 2   ac-

according to that Definition, neither Matter nor Spirit nor any
Finite Beings whatſoever, are
Subſtances, but only Modes; how
will it follow, that becauſe Subſtance is Self-exiſtent, therefore
all theſe Modes are ſo too ? Why,
becauſe † *from an In-*
finite Cauſe, Infinite
Effects muſt needs fol-
low. Very true ; ſup-
poſing That Infinite
Self-exiſtent Cauſe, not
to be a Voluntary, but
a mere Neceſſary Agent, that is,
no Agent at all ; Which Suppoſition (*in the preſent Argument*)
is the Queſtion begged ; And
what he *afterwards* attempts to
allege in proof of it, ſhall *af-*
terwards be conſidered in its proper place.

VIII. *The*

† Ex neceſſitate di-
vinæ naturæ infinita in-
finitis modis (hoc eſt,
omnia quæ ſub intelle-
ctum infinitum cadere
poſſunt,) ſequi debent.
Prop. 16.

VIII. *The Self-Existent and Ori-* *That the* *ginal Cause of all things, must be* *Self-ex-* *an Intelligent Being.* In this Pro- * istent Be-* position lies the main Question be- *be Intelli-* tween us and the Atheists. For *gent.* that Something must be Self-Ex- istent; and that That which is Self-Existent, must necessarily be Eternal and Infinite and the Ori- ginal Cause of all things; will not bear much dispute. But all Atheists, whether they hold the World to be *of it self* Eternal both as to the Matter and Form, or whether they hold the Matter on- ly to be Necessary and the Form Contingent, or whatever Hypo- thesis they frame, have always af- serted and must maintain, either directly or indirectly, that the Self-Existent Being is not an In- telligent Being, but either pure unactive Matter, or (which in o-

ther

ther Words is the very fame thing)
a mere Neceffary Agent. For a
mere Neceffary Agent muft of neceffity either be plainly and directly in the groffeft Senfe Unintelligent; which was the antient A-
theifts Notion of the Self-Exiftent
Being : or elfe its Intelligence
(which is the affertion of *Spinoza*
and fome Moderns,) muft be
wholly feparate from any Power
of Will and Choice ; which in
Refpect of any Excellency and
Perfection, or indeed to any common Senfe at all, is the very fame
thing.

Now that the Self-Exiftent Being, is not fuch a Blind and Unintelligent Neceffity, but in the moft
proper Senfe an Underftanding and
really Active Being , cannot indeed be Demonftrated ftrictly and
properly *a priori* ; becaufe we
know not wherein Intelligence confifts,

fifts, nor can fee the immediate and neceffary Connection of it with Self-Exiftence, as we can that of Eternity, Infinity, Unity, &c. But *a pofteriori*, almoft every thing in the World Demonftrates to us this great Truth, and affords undeniable Arguments to prove that the World, and all things therein, are the Effects of an Intelligent and Knowing Caufe.

And 1ft, Since in general there *Proved* are manifeftly in Things, various *from the Degrees* kinds of Powers and very differ- *of Perfe-* ent Excellencies and Degrees of *ction in* Perfection ; it muft needs be, that *Things, and the* in the Order of Caufes and Effects, *Order of Caufes* the Caufe muft always be more *and Ef-* Excellent than the Effect ; and *fects.* confequently the Self-Exiftent Being, whatever That be Suppofed to be, muft of neceffity (being the Original of all things) contain in it felf the Sum and higheft Degree of all the Perfections of all things. Not becauſe that which is Self-Exiſtent, muſt *therefore* have all poſſible Perfections : (For This, though moſt certainly true in it ſelf, yet cannot be ſo clearly demonſtrated *a priori* :) But becauſe it is impoſſible that any effect ſhould have any Perfection, which was not in the Cauſe : For if it had, then that Perfection would be cauſed by Nothing ; which is a flat Contradiction. Now an Unintelligent Being, 'tis evident, cannot be indued with all the Perfections of all things in the World. All things therefore cannot ariſe from an Unintelligent Original : and conſequently the Self-Exiſtent Being, muſt of Neceſſity be Intelligent.

There

There is no Possibility for an Atheist to avoid the Force of this Argument any other way, than by asserting one of these two things : Either that there is no Intelligent Being at all in the Universe ; or that Intelligence is no distinct Perfection, but merely a Composition of Figure and Motion, as Colour and Sounds are supposed to be. Of the former of which, every Mans own Consciousness is an abundant Confutation : And that the latter, (in which the main strength of Atheism lies,) is most absurd and impossible, shall be shown immediately : Which nevertheless if it could be supposed to be True, yet that even upon That Supposition it would still follow that the Self-Existing Being must needs be Intelligent, shall be proved in my 4th Argument upon this present Head.

Head. In the mean time, that it is moft abfurd and impoffible to fuppofe Intelligence not to be any diftinct Perfection, properly fpeaking, but merely a Compofition of Unintelligent Figure and Motion; will appear from what fhall be faid in the enfuing Argument, which is

From the Intelligence that is in created Beings. 2ly. Since *in Man in particular* there is undeniably that Power, which we call Thought, Intelligence, Confcioufnefs, Perception or Knowledge; there muft of Neceffity either have been from Eternity *without any Original Caufe at all,* an infinite Succeffion of Men, whereof *no one* has had a *Neceffary,* but *every one a Dependent and Communicated* Being; or elfe thefe Beings, indued with Perception and Confcioufnefs, muft at fome time or other have arifen purely out of that which had

had no fuch Quality as Senfe, Perception or Confcioufnefs , or elfe they muft have been produced by fome *Intelligent* Superiour Being. There never was nor can be any Atheift whatfoever, that can deny but that One of thefe three Suppofitions muft be the Truth : If therefore the two former can be proved to be falfe and impoffible, the latter muft be owned to be Demonftrably true. Now that the firft is impoffible, is evident from what has been already faid in proof of the *Second* General Head of this Difcourfe. And that the fecond is likewife impoffible ; may be thus Demonftrated. If Perception or Intelligence, be a *diftinct Quality* or Perfection , and not a mere Effect or Compofition of Unintelligent Figure and Motion ; then Beings indued with Perception and Confciouf-

sciousness, can never have arisen
purely out of that which had no
such Quality as Perception or
Consciousness; because nothing
can ever give to another any Perfection, that it hath not either
actually in it self, or at least in a
higher degree : *But* Perception or
Intelligence, is a distinct Quality
or Perfection , and not a meer
Effect or Composition of Unintelligent Figure and Motion. *First,*
If Perception or Intelligence, be any
real, distinct Quality or Perfection;
and not a meere Effect or Composition
of Unintelligent Figure and Motion,
then Beings indued with Perception
or Consciousness, can never possibly
have arisen purely out of that which
it self had no such Quality as Per-
ception or Consciousness , because
nothing can ever give to another any
Perfection, that it hath not either
actually in it self, or at least in a
higher

higher degree. This is very evident; becaufe if any thing could give another any Perfection which it has not it felf, that Perfection would be caufed abfolutely by *Nothing*; which is a flat Contradiction. If any one here replies, (as Mr. *Gildon* has done * in a Letter to Mr. *Blount,*) that Colours, Sounds, Tafte, and the like, arife from Figure and Motion, which have no fuch Qualities in themfelves; or that Figure, Divifibility, and other Qualities of Matter are confeffed to be given it by God, who yet cannot without extreme Blafphemy be faid to have any fuch Qualities himfelf; and that therefore in like manner Perception or † Intelligence may arife out of that which has no Intelligence it felf: The Anfwer is very eafie:

* *Oracles of Reafon,* pag. 186.

† If with one of *Cicero*'s Dialogifts they would infer that the whole muft have Underftanding, becaufe fome Portions of it are fiift,

Intelligent ; —— we may retort with the other Speaker in *Cicero,* that by the same Argument, the Whole must be a Courtier, a Musician, a Dancing-Master, or a Philosopher, because many of the Parts are such. Mr. *Toland's* Letter, *Motion essential to Matter.*

first , That Colours, Sounds , Taste , and the like, are by no means Effects arising from mere Figure and Motion ; there being nothing in the Bodies themselves , the Objects of the Senses, that has any manner of Similitude to any of these Qualities ; but they are plainly *Thoughts* or Modifications of the Mind it self, which is an Intelligent Being ; and are not properly *Caused,* but only *Occasioned,* by the Impressions of Figure and Motion : Nor will it at all help an Atheist (as to the present Question,) though we make for, his sake (that we may allow him the greatest possible Advantage) even That most absurd Supposition, that the Mind it self is nothing
but

but mere Matter, and not at all
an Immaterial Subſtance, For even
ſuppoſing it to be mere Matter, yet
he muſt needs confeſs it to be ſuch
Matter, as is indued not only with
bare Figure and Motion, but alſo with the Quality of Intelligence and Perception ; and then,
as to the preſent Queſtion, it will
ſtill come to the ſame thing ;
that Colours, Sounds, and the
like, which are not Qualities of
Unintelligent Bodies, but Perceptions of Mind, can no more be
cauſed by, or ariſe from, mere
Unintelligent Figure and Motion,
than Colour can be a Triangle,
or Sound a Square, or Something
be cauſed by Nothing. And then,
as to the Second Part of the Objection ; that Figure, Diviſibility,
and other Qualities of Matter are
(as we our ſelves acknowledge)
given it by God, who yet cannot
with-

without extreme Blasphemy be said to have any such Qualities himself, and that therefore in like manner Perception or Intelligence may arise out of that which has no Intelligence it self; The Answer is still easier; That Figure, Divisibility, and other such like Qualities of Matter, are not real, proper, distinct and Positive Powers, but only Negative Qualities, Deficiencies or Imperfections; and tho' no Cause can communicate to its Effect any real Perfection which it has not it self, yet the Effect may easily have many Imperfections or Negative Qualities which are not in the Cause. Though therefore Figure, Divisibility and the like, (which are mere Negations, as all Limitations are,) may be in the Effect, and not in the Cause; yet Intelligence, (which we now suppose, and shall prove imme-

immediately, to be a diftinct Quality; and which no Man can fay is a mere Negation;) cannot poffibly be fo. And now, having thus demonftrated, that if Perception or Intelligence be fuppofed to be a *diftinct Quality* or Perfection, (though even but of *Matter* only, if the Atheift pleafes,) and not a mere Effect or Compofition of Unintelligent Figure and Motion; then Beings indued with Perception or Confcioufnefs, can never have rifen purely out of that which had no fuch Quality as Perception or Confcioufnefs; becaufe nothing can ever give to another any Perfection, which it has not it felf: It will eafily appear, *fecondly,* That *Perception or Intelligence is really fuch a diftinct Quality or Perfection, and not poffibly a mere Effect or Compofition of Unintelligent Figure and Motion:* And

I that

that for this plain Reason; because Intelligence *is not* Figure, and Consciousness *is not* Motion. For whatever can arise from, or be compounded of any Things; is still only those very Things, of which it was compounded: And if infinite Compositions or Divisions be made eternally, the Things will still be but eternally the same: And all their possible Effects, can never be any thing but Repetitions of the same. For instance; All possible Changes, Compositions or Divisions of *Figure*, are still nothing but *Figure*: And all possible Compositions or Effects of *Motion*, can eternally be nothing but mere *Motion*. If therefore there ever was a Time, when there was nothing in the Universe but Matter and Motion; there never could have been any thing else therein, but Matter and Motion; And it would

have

have been as impoſſible, there
ſhould ever have exiſted any ſuch
thing as Intelligence or Conſciouſneſs; or even any ſuch thing as
Light, or Heat, or Sound, or Colour, or any of thoſe we call Secondary Qualities of Matter; as
it is now impoſſible for Motion to
be Blue or Red, or for a Trian-
angle to be transformed into a
Sound. That which has been apt
to deceive Men in this matter, is
this, that they imagine Compounds to be ſomewhat really
different from that of which they
are compounded : Which is a
very great Miſtake. For all the
Things, of which Men ſo judge;
either, if they be really different,
are not Compounds nor Effects of
what Men judge them to be, but
are ſomething totally diſtinct; as
when the Vulgar thinks Colours
and Sounds to be Properties Inhe-

rent

rent in Bodies, when indeed they are purely Thoughts of the Mind: Or elfe, if they be really Compounds and Effects, then they are not different, but exactly the fame that ever they were; as when two Triangles put together make a Square, that Squaie is ftill nothing but two Triangles; or when a Square cut in halves makes two Triangles, thofe two Triangles are ftill only the two halves of a Square, or when the mixtuie of Blew and Yellow Powder makes a Green, that Green is ftill nothing but Blew and Yellow intermixed, as is plainly vifible by the help of Microfcopes: And, in fhort, every thing by Compofition, Divifion, or Motion; is nothing elfe but the very fame it was before, taken either in whole or by Parts, or in different Place or Order. Mr. *Hobbs* feems to have been aware

of

of this : And therefore, though he is very sparing, and as it were a-shamed to speak out ; yet finding himself pressed in his own Mind with the Difficulty arising from the Impossibility of Sense or Con-sciousness being merely the Ef-fect of Figure and Motion ; and it not serving *his* Purpose at all, (were the thing never so possible,) to suppose that God by an imme-diate and voluntary Act of his *Almighty* Power indues certain Sy-stems of Matter with Conscious-ness and Thought, (of which O-pinion I shall have occasion to speak somewhat more hereafter ;) he is forced * to re-cur to that prodigi-ously absurd Supposi-tion, that All Matter, as Matter, is indued not only with Figure and a Capacity of Mo-tion,

* Scio fuisse Philo-sophos quosdam, eos-demq, *viros doctos*, qui corpora omnia Sensu prædita esse sustinue-runt : *nec video*, si na-tura sensionis in rea-ctione sola collocare-tur, *quomodo refutari*

I 3

poſſint. Sed etſi ex reactione etiam corporum
aliorum phantaſma ali-
quod naſceretur, illud
tamen remoto objecto
ſtatim ceſſaret : Nam
niſi ad retinendum mo-
tum impreſſum, etiam
remoto objecto, apta
habeant Organa, ut
habent Animalia; ita
tantum ſentient, ut nunquam ſenſiſſe ſe recordentur.....
Senſioni ergo, quæ vulgo ita appellatur, neceſſario adhæret memoria aliqua, &c. *Hobbs Phyſic.* *Cap.* 25.
Sect. 5.

tion, but alſo with
an actual Senſe or Per-
ception ; and wants
only the Organs and
Memory of Animals,
to expreſs its Senſati-
tion.

From the Beauty, Order, and final Cauſes of Things. 3dly, That the Self-exiſtent and Original Cauſe of all things, is an Intelligent Being ; appears abun-dantly from the excellent *Varie-ty, Order, Beauty* and *Wonderful Contrivance* and *Fitneſs* of all things in the *World*, to their proper and reſpective *Ends*. This Argument has been ſo Learnedly and Fully handled, both by Ancient and Mo-dern Writers ; that I do but juſt mention it, without inlarging at all

all upon it. I shall only at this Time make this One Observation: That whereas *Des Cartes* and others have indeavoured to give a Possible Account, how the World might be formed by the Necessary Laws of Motion alone; they have by so seemingly Vast an Undertaking, really meant no more, than to explain Philosophically how the inanimate part, that is, infinitely the least considerable part of the World, might possibly have been framed: For as to Plants and Animals, in which the Wisdom of the Creator principally appears; they have never in any tolerable manner, or with any the least appearance of Success, pretended to give an Account, how *They* were originally Formed. In these Things, Matter and the Laws of Motion, are able to do nothing at all: And how ridiculous the Epicurean Hy-

I 4   pothesis

pothesis is, of the Earth producing them all at first by chance,
(besides that I think it is now given
up, even by all Atheists,) appears
from the late Discovery made in
Philosophy, that there is no such
thing as equivocal Generation
of any the meanest Animal or
Plant ; the Sun and Earth and
Water, and all the Powers of Nature in Conjunction, being able to
do nothing at all towards the pro
ducing any thing indued with so
much as even a Vegetable Life:
(From which most excellent Discovery, we may *by the by* observe
the Usefulness of Natural and Ex-
perimental Philosophy, sometimes
even in Matters of Religion.)
Since therefore things are thus, it
must unavoidably be granted (e-
ven by the most Obstinate Atheist,)
either that all Plants and Animals
are originally the Work of an
In-

Intelligent Being, and Created by him in Time; or that having been from Eternity in the fame Order and Method they now are in, they are an Eternal Effect of an Eternal Intelligent Caufe continually exerting his Infinite Power and Wifdom; or elfe that without any Self-exiftent Original at all, they have been derived one from another in an Eternal Succeffion, by an infinite Progrefs of Dependent Caufes: The firft of thefe three ways, is the Conclufion we affert: The fecond, (fo far as the Caufe of Atheifm is concerned,) comes to the very fame thing: And the third I have already fhown, (in the Proof of the Second General Head of this Difcourfe,) to be abfolutely Impoffible and a Contradiction.

4*thly*,

4*thly*, Suppoſing it was poſſible that the Form of the World and all the Viſible things contained therein, with the Order, Beauty, and exquiſite Fitneſs of their Parts ; nay, ſuppoſing that even Intelligence it ſelf, with Conſciouſneſs and Thought, in all the Beings we know, could poſſibly be the Reſult or Effect of mere Unintelligent Matter, Figure and Motion : (which is the moſt unreaſonable and impoſſible Suppoſition in the World :) Yet even ſtill there would remain an undeniable Demonſtration, that the Self-exiſtent Being, (whatever it be ſuppoſed to be,) muſt be Intelligent. For even theſe Principles themſelves [*Unintelligent Figure* and *Motion*] could never have poſſibly exiſted without there having been before them an Intelligent Cauſe. I inſtance in *Motion*.

'Tis

'Tis evident there is Now such a thing as Motion in the World : Which either began at some Time or other, or was Eternal : If it began at any Time, then the Question is granted, that the First Cause is an Intelligent Being ; For mere Unintelligent Matter, and that at Rest, 'tis manifest could never of it self begin to Move: On the contrary, if Motion was Eternal, either it was eternally caused by some Eternal Intelligent Being ; or it must of it self be Necessary and Self-existent ; or else, without any Necessity in its own Nature, and without any External Necessary Cause, it must have existed from Eternity by an Endless Successive Communication : If Motion was eternally Caused by some Eternal Intelligent Being ; this also is granting the Question, as to the present Dispute : If it

was

was of it self Neceffary and Self-exiftent, then it follows, that it muft be a Contradiction in Terms, to fuppofe any Matter to be at Reft, And it muft alfo imply a Contradiction, to fuppofe that there might *poffibly* have been originally more or lefs Motion in the Univerfe than there *actually* was; which is fo very abfurd a Confequence, that *Spinoza* himfelf, though he exprefly afferts all Things to be *Neceffary*, yet

* Spinozæ Ethic. Par. I. Prop. 23. *compared with* Par. II. Prop. 13. Lemma 3.

feems afhamed * to fpeak out his Opinion, or rather plainly contradicts himfelf in the Queftion about the Original of Motion: But if it be faid that Motion, without any Neceffity in its own Nature, and without any External Neceffary Caufe, has exifted from Eternity, merely by an Endlefs Succeffive Communication;

tion; as † *Spinoza,* inconsistently enough, seems to assert; This I have before shown, (in the Proof of the Second General Proposition of this Discourse,) to be a flat Contradiction. It remains therefore, that Motion must of Necessity be Originally Caused by Something that is Intelligent; or else there never could have been any such Thing as Motion in the World: And consequently the Self-existent Being, the Original Cause of all Things, (whatever it be supposed to be,) must of Necessity be *an Intelligent Being.*

From hence it follows again, that the material World, cannot possibly be the Original Self-Existent

† Corpus motum vel quiescens, ad motum vel quietem determinari debuit ab alio corpore, quod etiam ad motum vel quietem determinatum fuit ab alio, & illud iterum ab alio, & sic *in infinitum.* Ethic. Par. II. Prop. 13. *Lemma* 3.

istent Being.   For since the Self-Existent Being, is demonstrated to be Intelligent; and the Material World plainly is not so, it follows that the Material World cannot possibly be Self-Existent. What some have fondly imagined concerning *a Soul of the World*; if thereby they mean a Created, Dependent Being; signifies nothing in the present Argument: But if they Understand thereby Something Necessary and Self-Existent, then it is nothing else, but a false, corrupt, and imperfect Notion of *God*.

That the Self-existent Being must be a Free Agent. **IX.** *The Self-Existent and Original Cause of all Things, is not a necessary Agent, but a Being indued with Liberty and Choice.* The contrary to this Proposition, is the Foundation and the Sum of

what

what *Spinoza* and his Followers have afferted, concerning the Nature of God. What Reafons or Arguments they have offered for their Opinion, I fhall have occafion to confider briefly in my Proof of the Propofition it felf. The Truth of which, appears

1st In that it is a Neceffary Confequence of the foregoing Propofition. For *Intelligence* without *Liberty* (as I there hinted) is really (in refpect of any Power, Excellence, or Pefection,) *no Intelligence* at all. It is indeed a *Confcioufnefs,* but it is merely *a Paffive One*; a Confcioufnefs, not of Acting, but purely of being Acted upon. Without Liberty, nothing can in any tolerable Propriety of Speech, be faid to be an Agent or Caufe of any thing. For to Act neceffarily, is really

This a neceffary Confequent of the foregoing Propofition.

and

and properly not to Act at all, but only to be Acted upon. What therefore *Spinoza* and his Followers affert concerning the Production of all Things *

* Ex neceffitate Divinæ naturæ, infinita, infinitis modis fequi debent. *Ethic. Par.* I. *Prop.* 16.

from the Neceffity of the Divine Nature, is mere Cant and Words without any meaning at all. For if by the Neceffity of the Divine Nature they underftand not the Perfection and Rectitude of his Will, whereby God is unalterably determined to do always what is beft in the whole ; (as confeffedly they do not; becaufe this is confiftent with the moft perfect Liberty and Choice,) but on the contrary they mean an Abfolute and Strictly Natural Neceffity : It follows evidently, that when they fay God, by the Neceffity of his Nature, is the Caufe

and

and Author of all things, they underſtand him to be a Cauſe or Agent in no other Senſe, than as if a Man ſhould ſay that a Stone, by the Neceſſity of its Na-ture, is the Cauſe of its own falling and ſtriking the Ground ; which is really not to be an Agent or Cauſe at all ; but their Opinion a-mounts to this, that all things are equally Self-Exiſtent, and conſe-quently that the Material World is God ; which I have before proved to be a Contradiction. In like manner, when they ſpeak of the Intelligence and Knowledge of God ; they mean to attribute theſe Powers to him in no other Senſe, than the *Hylozoicks* attri-buted them to all Matter ; that is, that a Stone, when it falls, has a Senſation and Conſciouſneſs ; but That Conſciouſneſs is no Cauſe at all, or Power of Acting.

K   Which

Which kind of Intelligence, in any tolerable Propriety of Speech, is no Intelligence at all : And Confequently the Arguments that proved the Supreme Caufe to be *properly* an Intelligent and Active Being, do alfo undeniably prove that he is likewife indued with Liberty and Choice, which alone is the Power of Acting.

Proved further from the Arbitrary Difpofition of Things in the World, with an Anfwer to Spinoza's Arguments for the Neceffity of all Things. 2*ly*, If the Supreme Caufe, is not a Being indued with Liberty and Choice, but a mere Neceffary Agent, whofe Actions are all as abfolutely and naturally Neceffary as his Exiftence : Then it will follow, that nothing which is not, could *poffibly* have been ; and that nothing which is, could *poffibly* not have been ; and that no Mode or Circumftance of the Exiftence of any thing, could *poffibly* have been in any refpect otherwife, than it now actually is.

All

All which, being evidently moſt false and abſurd : it follows on the contrary, that the Supreme Cauſe is not a mere neceſſary Agent, but a Being indued with Liberty and Choice. * The Conſequence ; that if the Supreme

** Alii putant, Deum eſſe cauſam liberam, propterea quod poteſt, ut putant, ef-*ficere ut ea quæ ex ejus natura ſequi diximus, hoc eſt, quæ *in ejus poteſtate ſunt,* non fiant; ſed hoc idem eſt ac ſi dicerent, quod Deus poteſt efficere, ut ex natura trianguli non ſequatur, ejus tres angulos æquales eſſe duobus rectis. ——Ego me ſatis clare oſtendiſſe puto, a ſumma Dei Potentia *Omnia* neceſſario effluxiſſe, vel ſemper eadem neceſſitate ſequi, eodem modo ac ex natura trianguli ab æterno & in æternum ſequitur, ejus tres angulos æquari duobus rectis. *Ethic. Par. I. Schol. ad Prop.* 17.

Omnia ex neceſſitate naturæ divinæ determinata ſunt, non tantum ad exiſtendum, ſed etiam ad certo modo exiſtendum & operandum, nullumq; datur Contingens. *Demonſtrat. Prop.* 29.

Si res alterius naturæ potuiſſent eſſe, vel alio modo ad operandum determinari; ut naturæ ordo alius eſſet : ergo Dei etiam natura alia poſſet eſſe quam jam eſt. *Prop.* 33. *Demonſtrat.*

Quicquid concipimus in Dei Poteſtate eſſe, id neceſſario eſt. *Prop.* 35.

Deum non operari ex libertate Voluntatis : *Corol. ad Prop.* 32.

Res nullo alio modo, neq; alio ordine a Deo produci potuerunt, quam productæ ſunt. *Prop.* 33.

Cauſe

Cauſe be a Neceſſary Agent, then nothing which is not, could *poſſibly* have been, and nothing which is, could *poſſibly* either not have been, or have been different from what 'tis; is expreſly owned by *Spinoza* to be the unavoidable Conſequence of his own Opinion : And accordingly he endeavours to maintain, that *no Thing, or Mode of Exiſtence of any Thing, could* poſſibly *have been in any reſpect different from what it now actually is* : His Reaſons are ; (1.) becauſe † *from an infinitely perfect Nature, infinite Things in infinite Manners, muſt needs proceed* ; and (2.) * *becauſe, if any thing could poſſibly be otherwiſe than it is, the Will and Nature of God muſt be ſuppoſed capable*

† Ex neceſſitate divinæ naturæ, infinita infinitis modis ſequi debent. *Prop.* 16.

* Si res alterius naturæ potuiſſent eſſe, vel alio modo ad operandum determinari ; ut naturæ Ordo alius eſſet . Ergo Dei etiam natura alia poſſet eſſe quam jam eſt. *Prop.* 33. *Demonſtrat.*

capable of change ; and
(3.) † *becaufe, if all*
poffible Things in all
poffible Manners do not
always and neceffarily
exift, they never can All
exift ; *but fome Things,*
that do not exift, will
ftill always be poffible
only ; *and fo the Actual*
Omnipotence of God is
taken away. The *firft*
of thefe Arguments, is
a plain begging the
Queftion : For, that
an Infinitely Perfect
Nature, *is able* indeed
to produce Infinite
Things in Infinite
Manners, is certainly true ; but
that it *muft always actnally* do fo
by an *abfolute Neceffity of Nature,*
without any Power of Choice, either as to Time or Manner or

† Imo adverfarii,[qui
negant, ex neceffitate
divinæ naturæ omnia
neceffario fluere,] Dei
Omnipotentiam negare
videntur. Coguntur
enim fateri, Deum in-
finita creabilia intelli-
gere, quæ tamen nun-
quam creare poterit.
Nam alias, fi fcilicet
omnia, quæ intelligit,
crearet ; fuam, juxta
ipfos, exhauriret Omni-
potentiam, & fe im-
perfectum redderet. Ut
igitur Deum perfe-
ctum ftatuant, eo redi-
guntur, ut fimul ftatu-
ere debeant, ipfum non
poffe omnia efficere,
ad quæ ejus potentia
fe extendit. *Coroll. ad*
Prop. 17.

K 3 Cir-

Circumſtances, does by no means
follow from the Perfection of its
Natuie, unleſs it be fiiſt *ſuppoſed*
to be a *Neceſſary Agent* ; which is
the very Queſtion begged, that was
to be proved. The *ſecond* Aigument,
is (if poſſible) ſtill weaker ; For
how does it follow, if God, according to his eternal unerring Purpoſe
and Infinite Wiſdom, produces
different Things at different Times
and in different Manners ; that
therefore the Will and Nature of
God, is changeable ? It might exactly as well be argued, that if
God (accoiding to *Spinoza*'s Suppoſition) does *Always* neceſſarily
produce all poſſible *Variety* of
Things ; therefore his Will and
Nature is *Always* neceſſarily infinitely *various*, *unequal*, and *diſſi-
milar to it ſelf.* And as to the
third Argument ; (beſides that 'tis
a mere Metaphyſical Vanity, and
ınakes

makes no difference between God's *actually and neceffarily doing* always all poffible Things in all poffible Manners, and his being *able to do them,*) it is juft fuch Reafoning, as if a Man fhould argue, that if all poffible [Eternal] Duration be not Always actually ex- haufted, it never can be All Ex- haufted; and that therefore fo the *Eternity* of God. is taken a- way. But whatever the Argu- ments were, and if they were ne- ver fo much more plaufible than they really are ; yet the Afferti- on it felf, [*viz : That no Thing, or Mode of Exiftence of any Thing, could* poffibly *have been made in any refpect different from what it actually is,*] is fo palpably abfurd and falfe, fo contradictory to ex- perience and the Nature of Things, and to the moft obvious and com- mon Reafon of Mankind ; that of

it

it self it immediately and upon the first hearing, sufficiently confutes any Principle of which it is a Consequence. For all Things in the World appear plainly to be the most Arbitrary that can be imagined; and to be wholly the Effects, not of *Necessity,* but of Wisdom and Choice. A *Necessity* indeed *of Fitness;* that is, that things could not have been Otherwise than they are, without diminishing the Beauty, Order, and well-Being of the Whole; there may be, and (as far as we can apprehend) there certainly Is: But this is so far from serving our Adversaries Purpose, that on the contrary 'tis a direct Demonstration that all things were made and ordered by a Free and a Wife Agent. That therefore which I affirm, contradictory to *Spinoza's* Assertion, is, That there is not

the

the leaft appearance of an *Abfolute Neceffity of Nature,* (fo as that any Variation would imply a Contradiction,) in any of thefe Things. *Motion* it felf, and all its Quantities and Directions, with the Laws of *Gravitation,* are intirely Arbitrary; and might poffibly have been altogether different from what they now are. The *Number* and *Motion* of the *Heavenly Bodies,* have no manner of Neceffity in the Nature of the Things themfelves. The number of the Planets might have been greater or lefs; And the Direction of all their Motions, both of the primary and fecondary Planets, uniformly from Weft to Eaft, when by the Motion of Comets it appears there was no Neceffity but that they might as eafily have moved in all imaginable tranfverfe Directions; is an evident proof

that

that theſe things are the Effect of Wiſdom and Choice. There is not the leaſt appearance of Neceſſity, but that all theſe things might poſſibly have been infinitely varied from their preſent Conſtitution, and (as the late improvements in Aſtronomy, diſcover) they *are* actually liable to very great Changes.   Every thing upon *Earth*, is ſtill more evidently arbitrary ; and plainly the Product, not of Neceſſity, but Will. What abſolute Neceſſity, for juſt ſuch a Number of *Species* of *Animals* or *Plants* ? or who without bluſhing dare affirm, that * neither the Form, nor Order, nor any the minuteſt Circumſtance or Mode of Exiſtence of any of theſe Things, could *poſſibly* have been in the leaſt diverſified by the Supreme Cauſe ?

* Res nullo alio modo, neq, alio Ordine, a Deo produci potuerunt, quam productæ ſunt. *Spinoza* ut ſupra.

To

To give but one Instance: In all the greater Species of Animals, Where was the Necessity for that conformity we observe in the Number and Likeness of all their Principal Members? and how would it have been a Contradiction, to suppose any or all of them varied from what they now are? To suppose indeed the continuance of such Monsters as *Lucretius* imagines to have perished for want of the principal Organs of Life, is really a Contradiction, But how would it have been a Contradiction for a whole Species of *Horses* or *Oxen*, to have subsisted with *Six Legs* or *Four Eyes*? But 'tis a shame to insist longer upon so plain an Argument.

It might have been Objected with much more Plausibleness, that the Supreme Cause cannot be be Free, becaufe He muft needs do always what is beft in the whole. But this would not at all ferve *Spinoza's* Purpofe. For this is a Neceffity, not of Nature and Fate, but of Fitnefs and Wifdom, a Neceffity, confiftent with the greateft Freedom and moft perfect Choice. For the only Foundation of this Neceffity, is fuch an unalterable Rectitude of Will and Perfection of Wifdom, as makes it impoffible for a Wife Being to refolve to Act Foolifhly; or for a Nature infinitely Good, to Choofe to do that which is Evil. *Of which I fhall have Occafion to fpeak more hereafter, when I come to Deduce the Moral Attributes of God.*

The fame proved alfo from Final Caufes 3*ly,* If there be any Final Caufe of any thing in the Univerfe; then the Supreme Caufe, is not a Neceffary, but a Free Agent.

This

This Confequence alfo, *Spinoza* acknowledges to be unavoidable: And therefore he has no other way left, but with a ftrange Confidence to †expofe all Final Caufes, as the Fictions of ignorant and fuperftitious Men: and to * laugh at thofe who are fo foolifh and childifh as to fancy that *Eyes* were defigned and fitted to *fee* with, *Teeth* to *chew* with, *Food* to be *eaten* for *Nourifh-ment*, the *Sun* to give light, &c. I fuppofe it will not be thought, that when once a Man comes to this, he is to be difputed with any longer. Whoever pleafes, may, for fatisfaction on this Head, confult *Galen de Ufu Partium, Tully de natura Deorum, Mr. Boyle of Final Caufes, and Mr. Ray*

† Naturam finem nullum fibi præfixum habere, & omnes caufas Finales, nihil, nifi humana effe Figmenta *Appendix ad Prop. 36.*

* Oculos ad Videndum, dentes ad mafticandum, herbas & animantia ad alimentum, folem ad illuminandum, mare ad alendum pifces, &c. *Ibid.*

Ray of the *Wisdom of God in the Creation.* I shall only observe this One Thing, that the greater the Improvements and Discoveries are, which are daily made in Astronomy and Natural Philosophy; the more clearly is this Question continually determined, to the Shame and Confusion of Atheists.

From the finiteness of Created Beings. 4thly, If the Supreme Cause be a mere Necessary Agent, it is impossible any Effect or Product of that Cause should be *Finite.* For since that which Acts necessarily, cannot govern or direct its own Actions; but must necessarily produce whatever can be the Effect or Product of its Nature: 'Tis plain, every Effect of such an Infinite Uniform Nature, acting every where necessarily alike; must of Necessity be Immense, or Infinite in Extension: And so no Crea-

Creature in the Universe, could possibly be Finite; which is infinitely Abfurd and contrary to Experience. *Spinoza,* to fhuffle off this Abfurdity, exprefles the Confequence of his Doctrine thus; That * *from the Necef-fity of the Divine Na-ture,* *infinite Things* (meaning infinite in number) *in infinite Man-ners muft needs follow :*

* Ex neceffitate divinæ naturæ, infinita infinitis modis fequi debent. *Ethic. Par. I, Prop. 16.*

But whoever reads his Demonftration of this Propofition, can hardly mifs to obferve, (if he be at all ufed to fuch Speculations,) that if it proved any thing at all, it would equally prove, That *from the Neceffity of the Divine Nature, Only Infinite Things* (meaning Infinite in Extenfion) *can poffibly arife.* Which Demonftration alone, is a fufficient Confutation of the Opinion it was defigned to eftablifh.

5*thly,*

5*thly.* If the Supreme Cause be not a Free and Voluntary Agent, then in every Effect, (for instance, in *Motion*,) there must have been a Progression of Causes *in infinitum*, without any Original Cause at all. For if there be no Liberty any where; then there is no Agent; no Cause, Mover, Principle, or Beginning of *Motion* any where : Every thing in the Universe must be *Passive*, and nothing *Active* ; Every thing *Moved*, and no *Mover* ; Every thing *Effect*, and nothing *Cause*. *Spinoza* indeed, (as has been already Observed) refers all things to *the Necessity of the Divine Nature*, as their real Cause and Original : But this is mere Cant, and Words without any Signification ; and will not at all help him over the present Difficulty. For if by Things Existing through the Necessity

ceſſity of the *Divine Nature,* he means *Abſolutely* a *Neceſſity of Exiſtence;* ſo as to make the World, and Every thing in it, *Self-Exiſtent;* then it follows (as I have before ſhown) that it muſt be a Contradiction in terms, to ſuppoſe *Motion,* &c, not to Exiſt; which *Spinoza* himſelf is aſhamed to aſſert. But if therefore by the *Neceſſity of the Divine Nature,* he means only the *Neceſſary following of an Effect from the Cauſe,* or, *the Cauſe neceſſarily producing its Effect;* this Neceſſity muſt ſtill always be determined by ſomething antecedent, and ſo on infinitely: And this, *Spinoza* (though ſometimes he ſeems to mean the other and equally abſurd Senſe) expreſſly owns in ſome Places to be his meaning: * *There can be no Voliti-* * *Una-quæq; Volitio non poteſt exiſtere, neq, ad operandum determinari; niſi ab alia cauſa determinetur, & hæc rurſus ab alia, & ſic porro in infinitum. Prop.* 32. *Dem.*

L   *on,*

on, ſaith he, *but from ſome Cauſe,*
which Cauſe muſt likewiſe be cauſed
by ſome other Cauſe, and ſo on in-
finitely. Again, *Will,*
† ſaith he, *belongs to the*
Nature of God, no o-
therwiſe than Motion
and Reſt do; So that
God can no more proper-
ly be ſaid to Act by the
Liberty of his Will,
than by the Liberty
of Motion and Reſt.
And what the Original of Motion and Reſt is, he tells us, in
theſe Words : * E-
very Body in Motion or
at Reſt, muſt have
been determined to that
Motion or Reſt by ſome
other Body, which muſt
it ſelf likewiſe have
been determined by a
third; and ſo on in in-
finitum

† Voluntas ad Dei naturam non magis pertinet, quam reliqua naturalia; ſed ad ipſam eodem modo ſeſe habet, ut motus & Quies.
Deus non magis dici poteſt ex libertate Voluntatis agere, quam dici poteſt ex libertate Motus & Quietis agere. *Coroll. ad Prop,* 32.

* Corpus motum vel quieſcens, ad motum vel quietem determinari debuit ab alio corpore, quod etiam ad motum vel quietem determinatum fuit ab alio; & illud iterum ab alio; & ſic in infinitum. *Ethic. Par.* II. *Prop.* 13. *Lemma* 3.

finitum. And thus, fince Motion is not in any one of its Stages of Communication *a Neceffary Self-exifting Being,* (becaufe the Body moved, may always without a Contradiction have been imagined to be at Reft, and is fuppofed not to have Motion from it felf, but from another;) the Opinion of *Spinoza* plainly recurs to *An Infinite Succeffion of dependent Beings produced one from another in an endlefs Progreffion, without any Original Caufe at all.* Which Notion I have already (in the Proof of the fecond General Head of this Difcourfe) Demonftrated to imply a Contradiction. And fince therefore there is no other poffible way to avoid this Abfurdity, but by granting that there muft be fomewhere a Principle of Motion and Action, which is Liberty; I fuppofe it by this time fufficiently

L 2   proved

proved, that the Supreme Cause must be a Being indued with Liberty and Choice.

That Liberty is not in it self an Impossible and contradictory Notion.

From what has been said upon this Head, it sufficiently appears, that Liberty is not in it self, and in the very Notion of the Thing, an absolute Contradiction and Impossibility; as the Pleaders for Necessity and Fate contend that it is, and place the chief strength of their Arguments in that Supposition. For that which actually is, is certainly not impossible : And it has already been proved, that Liberty actually is, nay, that it is impossible for it not to be, in the First and Supreme Cause. The Principal Argument used by the Maintainers of Fate against the Possibility of Liberty, is this: That since every thing must have a Cause, † every Voliti-

† *Mens ad hoc vel illud volendum determinatur a Causâ, quæ etiam ab alia determinata est, & hæc iterum ab alia, & sic in infinitum. Spinoza Ethic. Par. II. Prop. 48.*

on

on or Determination of the Will
of an Intelligent Being, muſt as
all other things, ariſe from ſome
Cauſe, and that Cauſe from ſome
other Cauſe, and ſo on infinitely. But this very Argument
really proves the direct contrary:
For ſince every thing muſt indeed have a Cauſe of its Being,
either from without, or in the
Neceſſity of its own Nature; and
it is a flat contradiction (as has already been demonſtrated) to ſuppoſe an infinite Series of dependent Effects, none of which are
Neceſſary in Themſelves or Self-
Exiſtent; therefore it is impoſſible but there muſt be in the Univerſe Some Being, whoſe Exiſtence is founded in the Neceſſity
of its Own Nature, and who Being acted upon by Nothing beyond it ſelf, muſt of Neceſſity have
in it ſelf a Principle of Acting, or

L 3   Power

Power of beginning Motion, which is the Idea of Liberty. 'Tis true, this Argument proves only the Liberty of the First and Supreme Cause ; and extends not indeed to any Created Being : But it evinces in General, (which is sufficient to my present purpose,) that Liberty is so far from being impossible and contradictory in it self, that on the contrary it is impossible but that it must really *Be* somewhere ; and this being once established, it will be easie to shew hereafter that it is a Power capable of being communicated to Created Beings ; of which in its proper place.

That the Self-existent Being, must be All-powerful.   X. *The Self-Existent Being, the Supreme Cause of all things, must of Necessity have Infinite Power.* This Proposition is evident, and unde-

undeniable. For since nothing (as has been already proved) can poffibly be Self-exiftent, befides Himfelf; and confequently all things in the Univerfe were made by Him, and are entirely dependent upon Him; and all the *Powers* of all Things are derived from Him, and muft therefore be perfectly Subject and Subordinate to Him: 'Tis manifeft that Nothing can make any Difficulty or Refiftance to the Execution of his Will; but he muft of neceffity have abfolute Power to do every thing he pleafes, with the perfecteft Eafe, and in the perfecteft Manner, at once and in a Moment, whenever he Wills it. The Defcriptions the Scripture gives of *this Power*, are fo lively and emphatical, that I cannot forbear mentioning one or two Paffages: Thus *Job* 9. 4. *He is wife in Heart, and mighty in Strength;----*

which

which removeth the Mountains, and
they know it not ; which overturn-
eth them in his Anger : Which sha-
·keth the Earth out of her place, and
the Pillars thereof tremble : which
commandeth the Sun, and it riseth not;
and Sealeth up the Stars : Which a-
lone spreadeth out the Heavens , and
treadeth upon the Waves of the Sea:
Which doth great things past
finding out , yea and Wonders
without number.   Again : Hell is
naked before him, and Destruction
hath no covering : He stretcheth out
the North over the empty place, and
hangeth the Earth upon nothing :
He bindeth up the Waters in his thick
Clouds, and the Cloud is not rent
under them : The Pillars of Heaven
tremble , and are astonished at his
Reproof : He divideth the Sea with
his Power, and by his Understanding he smiteth through the Proud :
Lo, these are part of his Ways, but
how

*how little a Portion is heard of him ?
but the Thunder of his Power, who
can understand ? Job 26. 6. So
likewise, Isaiah 40. 12. Who has
measured the Waters in the hollow of
his Hand ? and meted out Heaven
with the Span ? and comprehended
the Dust of the Earth in a Measure ?
and weighed the Mountains in Scales,
and the Hills in a Balance ? Behold,
the Nations are as a drop of the
Bucket, and are counted as the small
Dust of the Balance ; behold, he
taketh up the Isles, as a very little
thing : All Nations before him are
as nothing, and they are counted to
him less than nothing and Vanity :
To whom then will ye liken God, or
what likeness will ye compare unto
him ?* I do not urge Authority to
the Persons I am at present speaking to : But 'tis evident from *Reason,* that the Supreme Cause must
of Necessity be Infinitely Powerful.

The

The only Question is, what the true meaning of what we call *Infinite Power* is, and to what things it must be understood to extend, or not to extend.

Now in determining this Question, there are some Propositions, about which there is no dispute. Which therefore I shall but just mention : As

Of working Contradictions.

1*st.* That infinite Power reaches all *Possible* things ; but cannot be said to extend to the working any thing which implies a Contradiction : As, that a Thing should *be* and *not be* at the same time ; that the same thing should *be made* and *not be made,* or *have been* and *not have been* ; that *twice two* should *not make four,* or that *That which is necessarily False,* should *be True.* The Reason whereof is plain : Because a Power of making a Thing to be, at the same time that it is not ;

not; is only a Power of doing that which is Nothing, that is, no Power at all.

2*dly.* Infinite Power cannot be said to extend to thofe things, *O, Natural and Moral Evils.* which imply *Natural* Imperfection in the Being to whom fuch Power is afcribed : As, that it fhould deftroy its own Being, weaken it felf, or the like. Thefe Things imply *Natural* Imperfection ; and are by all Men confeffed to be fuch, as cannot poffibly belong to the Neceffary Self-exiftent Being. There are alfo other things which imply Imperfection in another kind, *viz. Moral* Imperfection : Concerning which, Atheifm takes away the Subject of the Queftion, by denying wholly the Difference of Moral Good and Evil; and therefore I fhall omit the Confideration of them, till I come to deduce the *Moral* Attributes of God.

But

But some other Instances there are, in the Question about the Extent of *Infinite Power*; wherein the Principal Difference between us and the Atheists, (next to the Question, whether the Supreme Cause be an *Intelligent Being*, or not,) does in a great measure consist. As

Of the Power of Creating Matter. 1*st*. That Infinite Power includes a Power of Creating Matter. This has been constantly denied by all Atheists, both Antient and Modern; and as constantly affirmed by all who believe the Being, and have just Notions of the Attributes of God. The only Reason which the Atheists have, or can pretend to allege for *their* Opinion; is, that the Thing is in its own Nature absolutely *Impossible*. But how does it appear to be impossible? Why, Only because They are not able to comprehend *How* it can be. For, to reduce it to a

Con-

Contradiction, (which is the alone real Impoſſibility,) this they are by no means able to do. For to ſay, that Something which once was not, may ſince have begun to exiſt ; is neither directly, nor by any Conſequence whatſoever, to aſſert that That which *is not,* can *be,* while it *is* Not; or that That which *is,* can *Not be,* while it *is.* 'Tis true, We, who have been uſed to Converſe only with Generations and Corruptions ; and never ſaw any thing *Made* or *Created,* but only *Formed* or *Framed*; are apt to indeavour to conform our Idea of *Creation,* to that of *Formation*; and to imagine, that as in all *Formations* there is ſome Præexiſting *Matter,* out of which a thing is *Formed*; ſo in *Creation* there muſt be conſidered a Præ-exiſtent *Nothing,* *out of* which, as out of a real *Material* Cauſe, a thing is *Created*; which looks indeed

deed like a Contradiction : But this is only a Confusion of Idea's ; just like Childrens imagining that Darkness is some real thing, which in the Morning is driven away by the Light, or transformed into it : Whereas the true Notion of Creation, is not a *Forming* Something *Out of* Nothing, as out of a *Material Cause* ; but only a Bringing Something into Being, that before had no Being at all ; or a Causing Something to Exist Now, that did not Exist Before ; or which without this Cause, would not have Existed : Which no Man can ever reduce to a Contradiction ; any more than the *Formation* of any thing into a Shape which it had not before, can be reduced to a Contradiction. And indeed, if they would speak out the Truth, the Sum of what all Atheists, whether Antient or Modern, have e-

ver

ver ſaid upon this Head, amounts
to no more but this One fooliſh Argument : That Matter could
not begin to exiſt, when *it was
not* ; becauſe this is ſuppoſing it
to Be, before it was : and that it
could not begin to Exiſt, when
it was ; becauſe this is ſuppoſing
it not to Be, after it was. Which
is juſt ſuch an Argument, as That
whereby a Certain Philoſopher
Demonſtrated, that there can be
no ſuch thing as *Motion* at all ; becauſe a Body can neither move
in the Place where *it is*, nor in
the place where *it is not*. The
Arguments are exactly alike : And
the ſame Anſwer will ſerve in-
differently for them Both.

2*ly.* 'Tis Poſſible to Infinite *Of the*
Power, to Create an *Immaterial* *Power of*
Cogitative Subſtance, indued with *Creating*
Immate-
a Power of beginning Motion, and *rial Co-*
with a *Liberty of Will or Choice.* *gitative*
Subſtan-
This *ces.*

This also has been always denied by all Atheists. And because it is a Proposition of the greatest Consequence to Religion and Morality, therefore I shall be particular in endeavouring the Proof of the several Parts of it.

First then, it is possible to infinite Power, to Create an *Immaterial* Cogitative Substance. That there can be such a Thing as a Cogitative Substance, that is, a Substance indued with Consciousness and Thought, is granted by all; because every Man's own Experience convinces him, that He himself is such a Substance. Further, That if there be, or can be, any such thing as Immaterial Substances; that then it is most reasonable to Believe, that such Substances as are indued with Consciousness and Thought, [Properties the farthest distant from the known Proper-

Properties of Matter, and the most unlike them, that can possibly be imagined,] are those Immaterial Substances; will also, I think, be granted by all Men. The only thing therefore, that remains to be proved, is this; That *Immaterial* Substances are not impossible, or, That a Substance *Immaterial* is not a contradictory Notion. Now whoever asserts that it is contradictory; must affirm, that whatever is not Matter, is nothing; and that to say Any thing Exists which is not Matter, is saying that there Exists something which is nothing. Which in Other Words is plainly this; That whatever we have no Idea of, is nothing, and impossible to Be. -For there is no other way to reduce *Immaterial* Substance to a Contradiction, but by supposing *Immaterial* to Signifie the

M   same

same as *Having no Existence* ; And there is no possible way to prove That, but by saying we have no Idea of it, and therefore it neither has nor can have any Existence. By which same Argument (even supposing it true, which yet is indeed most false, that we have a clear Idea of the Essence of Matter, aud none at all of any Immaterial Substance,) a Man Born Blind may Demonstrate irrefragably, that *Light* or *Colour* is an Impossible and Contradictory Notion, because it is not a *Sound* or a *Smell*. For the Power of *seeing Light or Colour*, is to a Man Born Blind, altogether as incomprehensible and absolutely beyond the Reach of all his Ideas, as either the Operations and Perceptions, or even the Simple Essence of a Pure Immaterial Substance or Spirit, can be to

any

any of Us. If therefore the Blind Mans want of Idea's be not a sufficient Proof of the Impossibility of Light or Colour ; how comes our bare want of Idea's, to be a Demonstration of the Impossibility of the Being of Immaterial Substances ? A Blind Man, they will say, has *Testimony* of the Existence of Light : Very true ; so also have we, of the Existence of Immaterial Substances : But, I hope, an Atheist will not put the Issue of his Cause upon *Testimony*, whatever he does. But there is this further advantage on our side in the Comparison; that a Blind man, excepting the Testimony of *Others*, finds not by any reasoning with himself, the least likelihood or probability, no not in the lowest possible degree, that there can be any such thing as Light or Colour ; But we, besides Testi-

mony,

mony, have great and ftrong Arguments both from Experience
and Reafon, that there are fuch
things as Immaterial Subftances,
though we have no Knowledge
of their Simple Effence. Even
the very firft and moft univerfal
Principle of Gravitation it felf in
all inanimate Matter; fince it is e-
ver Proportional, not at all to the
Surfaces of Bodies or of their Par-
ticles in any poffible Suppofition,
but entirely to the *Solid Content* of
Bodies; 'tis evident it cannot be
caufed by Matter acting upon the
Surfaces of Matter, which is all *It*
can do; but muft be caufed by
fomething which continually penetrates its *Solid Subftance*. But
in *Animals*, which have a Power
of Self-motion; and in the perfecter Sorts of them, which have ftill
higher Faculties; the thing is yet
more evident. For we fee and feel
and

and obferve daily in our felves and others, fuch Powers and Operations and Perceptions, as undeniably evince themfelves either to be the Properties of Immaterial Subftances : Or elfe it will follow that Matter is Something, of whofe inmoft Subftance and Effential Powers we have altogether as little Idea, as we have of Immaterial Beings ; and then how are Immaterial Subftances more impoffible than Material ? But of this, more hereafter.

From what has been faid on this Head, it will be eafy to anfwer all the Objections that have been brought by any Atheifts, againft the Notion of Human Souls being Immaterial Subftances diftinct from Body. For fince 'tis poffible there may be fuch things as Immaterial Subftances ; and fince if any fuch Subftance *Can* Be,

Of the Immateriality of Human Souls.

M 3   there

there is all the Reason in the World to Believe that Conscious and Thinking Substance *Is* such, these Properties being the most Remote from the known Properties of Matter, that are possible to be conceived; The Foundation of all the Objections against the Immateriality of the Soul, is entirely taken away. I shall not now Tarry to Consider the Objections in particular, which have been often and fully answered by learned Pens, but shall only mention One, on which all the rest depend, and to which they may all be reduced. And it is This:

* That seeing the only means we have of Perception, are the Five Senses, and these all plainly depend upon the Organs of the Body; therefore the Soul

* ——Si immortalis natura animai est,
Et sentire potest secreta a corpore nostro;
Quinq; (ut opinor) eam faciundum est *Sensibus* auctam:
Nec ratione alia nosmet proponere nobis

Soul without the Body, can have no Perception, and consequently is Nothing. Now (besides that these very Senses or Perceptions, however they may be obstructed by bodily Indisposition, and so do indeed depend upon the Organs of the Body as to their present *Exercise*, yet in their *Nature* are really entirely distinct Powers, and cannot possibly, as has been before shown, be absolutely founded in, or arise from; any of the known Properties or Qualities of Matter: Besides this, I say;) of Him that thus argues, I would only ask this one Question: Are our Five Senses, by an

Possumus infernas animas Acherunte vagare :

Pictores itaq; & scriptorum secla priora

Sic animas introduxerunt sensibus auctas.

At neq; seorsum oculi, &c.----

Nec sensus ipsi seorsum consistere possunt

Naribus atq; manu, atq; oculis, atq, auribus, atq;

Lingua , nec per se possunt sentire , nec esse. *Lucret lib.* 3.

Ὅσων γάρ ἐςιν ἀρχῶν ἡ ἐνέργεια σωματικὴ, δῆλον ὅτι ταῦτα, ἄνευ σώματ᾽ ἀδύνατον ὑπάρχειν οἷον βαδίζειν ἄνευ ποδῶν. *Aristot.*

M 4   Abso-

Abſolute *Neceſſity* in the Nature of
the Thing, All and the only Poſſible Ways of Perception ? And is
it impoſſible and contradictory,
that there ſhould be any Being in
the Univerſe, indued with ways of
Perception different from theſe that
are the reſult of *Our* preſent Compoſition ? Or are theſe things on
the contrary purely *Arbitrary*;
and the ſame Power that gave *Us*
theſe, may have given Others to
Other Beings, and might (if he had
pleas'd) have given *Us* Others in
in this *preſent* State, and may yet
have made us capable of different
Ones in *Another* State ? If they
be purely *Arbitrary*; then the want
of theſe, does by no means infer
a total want of Perception ; but
the ſame Soul, which in the preſent
State has the Powers of *Reflexion,
Reaſon and Judgment*, which are
Faculties entirely different from

Senſe;

Senfe ; may as eafily in another State have different ways even of *Perception* alfo ; But if any one fay, that thefe Senfes of ours, are *Neceffarily* the only ways of Perception ; how does that appear ? And is it not infinitely more reafonable to fuppofe, that this is a * mere Prejudice ariſing from Cuftom and an attending to bare Senfe in oppofition to Reafon ? For fuppofe Men had been created only with Four Senfes, and had never known the ufe of *Sight*, would they not then have had the fame Reafon to conclude there were but *Four* poffible ways of Perception, as they have Now to fancy that there are but

† Has tamen imagines [*mortuorum*] *Loqui* volebant ; quod fieri nec fine lingua, nec fine palato, nec fine faucium, laterum, pulmonum vi & figura poteft. Nihil enim *Animo (fpeaking of fuch as attributed to Spirits the fame Powers and Senfes only, as they faw Men endued with in this prefent State,)* videre poterant : Ad *oculos* omnia referebant. Magni autem ingenii eft, revocare mentem a fenfibus, & cogitationem a Confuetudine abducere. *Cicero Tufcul. Quæf.* I.

Five ?

Five ? And would they not then have thought *Sight* to have been an Impoffible, Chimerical, and merely imaginary Power ; with abfolutely the *fame Reafon,* as they now prefume the Faculties of immaterial Beings to be fo ? that is, with *no Reafon at all.* One would think, Men fhould be afhamed therefore to be fo Vain, as merely from their own Negative *Ignorance,* without any appearance or pretence of any *Pofitive* Argument, to argue againft the *Poffibility* of the Being of Things, which (excepting Only that they cannot frame to themfelves an *Image* or *Notion* of them) there is a Concurrence of all the Reafons in the World to perfwade them that fuch Things Really are. And then as to the Difficulty of Conceiving the Nature and Manner of the *Union* between Soul and Body ;

dy : We know altogether as much of That, as we do of the Nature of the Union or Cohæsion of the infinitely divisible parts of Body to Body ; which yet no Man doubts of : And therefore our Ignorance can be no more an Argument against the Truth of the One, than it is a Bar to our Belief of the Other.

Secondly, It is possible to Infinite Power, to indue a Creature with *the Power of Beginning Motion.* This is constantly denied by all Atheists , because the Consequence of it, is a *Liberty of Will,* of which I shall have Occasion to speak presently. But that the Proposition is true, I thus prove. If the Power of Beginning Motion be in it self a *Possible Thing* ; and also be *Possible to be communicated* ; Then a Creature may be Indued with That Power. Now that

Of induing Creatures with the Power of beginning Motion.

that the Power of Beginning Motion is in it self a *Possible Thing*, I
have already proved, by showing
that there must *Necessarily* be
somewhere a Power of Beginning
motion, because otherwise *Moti-*
on must have been from Eternity,
without any *External* Cause of its
Being; and yet it is a Thing that
has no Necessity of Existence in its
own Nature : So that if there be
not *somewhere* a Principle or Power
of beginning Motion ; *Motion* must.
Exist, without any Cause or Reason at all of its Existence, either
within it self or *from without* ;
which, as I have before shown, is
an Express Contradiction : Wherefore a Principle or Power of Beginning Motion, there must of necessity *Be*, somewhere or Other ;
and Consequently it is not in it
self an Impossible thing. I add :
As a Power of Beginning Motion,

is not in it self an Impossible
Thing ; because it must of Necessity *Be* in the Supreme Cause : So
neither is it impossible to be *Com-*
municated to Created Beings. The
Reason is plain : Because no Powers are Impossible to be Communicated, but only those which
imply Self-Existence and Absolute
Independency. That a Subordinate Being should be Self-Existent
or absolutely Independent, is indeed a Contradiction ; but 'tis no
Contradiction to suppose it indued with any Other Power whatsoever, separate from these. I
know the Maintainers of Fate, are
very Confident that a Power of
Beginning Motion, is nothing less
than being really Independent, or
being able to Act Independently
from any Superior Cause. But
this is only a childish trifling with
Words. For a Power of Acting
in-

independently *in this Sense,* Communicated at the Pleasure of the Supreme Cause, and Continued only during the same good Pleasure, is no more a real and absolute Independency, than the Power of *Existing,* (which I suppose the Defenders of Fate are not so fond to make a Continual Creation, as they are to make the power of Self-Motion a Continual External Impulse,) or than the power of *being Conscious,* or any other *Power* whatsoever, can be said to imply Independency. In reality, 'tis altogether as hard to conceive, how *Consciousness* or the power of *Perception* should be communicated to a Created Being, as how the power of *Self-Motion* should be so : unless Perception be Nothing else but a meer Passive Reception of Impulse; which I suppose is as clear that it is not, as that a

Trian-

Triangle is not a Sound, or that a Globe is not a Colour. Yet no Man doubts, but that He Himself and all others have truly a Power of Perception : And therefore in like manner, (however hard it may be to Conceive, as to the manner of it; yet since, as has now been proved, it can never be shewn to be impossible and expresly contradictory, that a power of Self-Motion should be communicated,) I suppose no considering Man can doubt, but that he actually has also a Power of *Self-Motion.* For the Arguments drawn from continual Experience and Observation, to prove that we have such a Power, are so strong; that nothing less than a strict Demonstration that the thing is absolutely impossible and implies an express Contradiction, can make us in the least doubt that we have it not.

not. We have all the same Experience, the same Marks and Evidence exactly, of our having *Really* a power of Self-motion; that the rigidest Fatalist could possibly contrive to require, if he was to make a *Supposition* of a Man's being endued with that power : There is no One Thing, which such a Man can imagine ought to follow from the Supposition of Liberty, which every Man does not Now as much Feel and actually Experience in Himself, as it can possibly be imagined any Man would do, supposing the Thing were true. Wherefore to affirm, notwithstanding all this, that the Spirits by which a man moves the Members of his Body, and ranges the Thoughts of his Mind, are themselves moved wholly by Air or Subtler Matter inspired into the Body

Body; and That again by other external Matter, and so on; as the Wheels of a Clock are moved by the Weights, and those Weights by Gravitation, and so on; without a mans having the least power by any Principle within himself, to think any one Thought, or impell his own Spirits in order to move any Member of his Body; All this is so contrary to Experience and the Reason of Things, that unless the Idea of Self-motion were in it self as evidently and *Clearly* a Contradiction, as that two and two should make fifteen, a Man ought to be ashamed to talk at that Rate. Nay a Man of any considerable degree of Modesty, would even in that Case be almost tempted rather to doubt the Truth of his Faculties; than boldly assert one so intolerable an Absurdity, only to avoid another.

N

ther. There are ſome indeed, who denying Men the Power of *Beginning Motion*, would yet ſeem in ſome manner to account for their Actions, by allowing them a Power of *Determining* Motion. But this alſo is a mere ludicrous trifling with Words. For if that Power of *Determining* Motion be no other in a Man, than that which is in a Stone of Reflecting a Ball *one certain way*; this is juſt Nothing at all: But if he has a Power of *Determining* the Motion of his Spirits *any way*, as he himſelf pleaſes; this is in all Reſpects the very ſame as the Power of *Beginning Motion*.

Of the Poſſibility of induing a Creature with Freedom or Liberty of Will.　Thirdly, 'Tis Poſſible to Infinite Power, to indue a Creature with *Freedom or Liberty of Will*. It might ſuffice that this is at once proved by the ſame Arguments, and in the ſame Method, as I

juſt

juft now proved *Self-Motion* or a *Power of beginning Motion*, to be poffible: *viz*, Becaufe *Liberty* muft of neceffity *Be* in the Supreme Caufe, (as is at large proved in the *Ninth* General Head of this Difcourfe,) and therefore cannot be impoffible and contradictory in the Nature of the thing it felf : And becaufe it implies no Contradiction to fuppofe it *communicated*; as being no harder to conceive, than the forementioned Power of Beginning Motion : And becaufe the Arguments drawn from Experience and Obfervation, are ftronger on the one fide of the Queftion, than thofe arifing merely from the Difficulty of our apprehending the thing, can be on the other. But forafmuch as this is the Queftion of the greateft Concern of all, in Matters both of Religion and Humane Life ; and both *Spinoza* and Mr. *Hobbs*, and

their

their Followers, have with great Noise and Confidence denied it : I shall therefore, not contenting my self with this, indeavour to shew moreover, in particular, the weakness of the principal Arguments, by which these Men have pretended to demonstrate, that there cannot *possibly* be any such Power in Man, as a Liberty of Will.   As to the Propriety of the Terms, whether the Will be properly the Seat of Liberty or not, it is not now to the purpose to inquire : The Question being, not where the Seat of Liberty is ; but whether there be *at all* in Man any such Power, as a Liberty of Choice and of Determining his own Actions ; or on the contrary his Actions be all as Necessary, as the Motions of a Clock.   The Arguments by which *Spinoza* and Mr. *Hobbs* have attempted to maintain this latter

side

fide of the Queſtion, are all plainly reducible to theſe two.

1*ſt*. That ſince every Effect muſt needs be produced by ſome Cauſe; therefore as every Motion in a Body muſt have been cauſed by the Impulſe of ſome other Body, and the Motion of that by the Impulſe of a Third; ſo every Volition, or Determination of the Will of Man, muſt needs be produced by ſome External Cauſe, and that in like manner be the Effect of ſome Third : And conſequently that there cannot poſſibly be any ſuch Thing in Nature, as Liberty or Freedom of Will.

2*dly*. That Thinking, and all its Modes, as Willing and the like, are Qualities or Affections of Matter : and conſequently, ſince 'tis manifeſt that Matter has not in it ſelf a Power of Beginning Moti-

on,

on, or giving it self any manner of Determination whatsoever, therefore 'tis evident likewise that 'tis impossible there should be any such Thing as Freedom of Will.

An Answer to M. Hobs and Spinoza's Arguments against the Possibility of Liberty. Now to these Arguments I oppose, and shall endeavour briefly to Demonstrate, the three following Propositions.

1*st*. That every Effect cannot possibly be the product of external Causes, but there must of Necessity be Somewhere a Beginning of Operation, or a Power of Acting without being antecedently acted upon : And that this Power may be, and is, in *Man*.

2*dly*. That Thinking and Willing neither are, nor can be, Qualities or Affections of Matter ; and consequently not concluded under the Laws thereof.

3*dly* That

3*dly*. That even suppofing the Soul not to be a diftinct Subftance from Body, but that Thinking and Willing could be, and were indeed, only Qualities or Affections of Matter; yet even *This* would not at all Affect the prefent Queftion, nor prove Freedom of Will to be impoffible.

1*ft*. Every Effect cannot poffibly be the Product of external Caufes; but there muft of Neceffity be fomewhere a Beginning of Operation, or a Power of Acting without being antecedently acted upon: and this Power may be, and Is, in Man. The feveral parts of this Propofition have been already proved in the *Second* and *Ninth* General Heads of this Difcourfe, and in that part of this *Tenth* Head which is concerning the Poffibility of the Power of Self-Motion being communi-

That there muft be fome-where a Beginning of Operation.

N 4   cated

cated to Created Beings. I shall not therefore here repeat the Proofs; but only apply them to *Spinoza's* and Mr *Hobbs's* Arguments, so far as is necessary to show the weakness of what they have said upon this Head in Opposition to the Possibility of Liberty or Freedom of Will. The manner then of their Arguing upon this Head, is this. *That Every Effect must needs be owing to some Cause; and That Cause must produce the Effect* [*] *necessarily; because if it be a sufficient Cause, the Effect cannot but follow, and if it be not a sufficient Cause, it will not be at*

[*] Quicunq; unquam Effectus productus sit, productus est a causa necessaria. Nam quod productum est, eo ipso quod productum est causam habuit integram, hoc est, omnia ea quibus suppositis Effectum non sequi intelligi non possit : ea vero causa necessaria est. *Hobbs Philosophia prima, cap. 9.*

all

all a Cause of that Thing : Thus, for instance, † *whatever Body is moved, must be moved by some other Body, which it self likewise must be moved by some Third, and so on without End :* That the ‖ *Will, in like manner, of any voluntary Agent, must of necessity be determined by some external Cause, and not by any Power*

† Corpus motum vel quiescens ad motum vel Quietem determinari debuit ab alio corpore, quod etiam ad motum vel Quietem determinatum fuit ab alio, & illud iterum ab alio, & sic in infinitum. *Spinoza E-thic. Par.* II. *Prop.* 13. *Lemma* 3.

‖ Unaquæque Volitio non potest Existere, neque ad operandum determinari, nisi ab alia causa determinetur, & hac rursus ab alia; & sic porro in infinitum.

Id Ethic. Par I *Prop:* 32. *Demonstrat.*

I conceive, nothing taketh beginning from it self, but from the Action of some immediate Agent without it self And that therefore when first a Man had an Appetite or Will to something, to which immediately before he had no Appetite or Will, the Cause of his Will is not the Will it self, but something else not in his own disposing. *Hobbs's Debate with Bp. Bramhall,* p. 239.

In mente nulla est absoluta sive libera voluntas; sed mens ad hoc vel illud volendum determinatur a causa, quæ etiam ab alia determinata est, & hæc iterum ab alia, & sic in infinitum. *Spinoza, Ethic. Par.* II. *Prop.* 48.

of

of determining it self, inherent in it self; And That External Cause must be determined necessarily by some other Cause, External to It ; and so on without End.   From all which it evidently appears, that All that these Men urge against the Possibility of Freedom, extends equally to all other Beings (not excepting the *Supreme*) as well as to Men ; and † *Spinoza* in express Words confesses it : Wherefore consequently,   whatever noise they make of the mighty Strength and Demonstrative Force of their Arguments, All that they say, amounts to no more but this One most Absurd Conclusion, That *there is no where, nor can possibly be, any Principle of Motion or Beginning of Operation at all* ; *but every thing is caused necessarily by an eternal Chain of Dependent Causes*

† Hinc sequitur, *Deum* non operari ex libertate Voluntatis. *Ethic. Par.* I. *Coroll. ad Prop.* 32.

ses and *Effects, without any Indepen-*
dent Original. All their Arguments
therefore on this Head, are al-
ıeady anfwered in the *Second* and
Ninth General Heads of this Difcourfe ; (where I proved that
there muft of neceffity be an *Ori-*
ginal, Independent, and *Free* Principle of Motion or Action ; and
that to fuppofe an endlefs Succef-
fon of Dependent Caufes and Effects, without any Original or
Firft and Self-actuating Principle,
is fuppofing a *Series* of *dependent*
Things to be *from Eternity* produced by *Nothing* ; which is the very fame Abfurdity and Contradiction, as to fuppofe Things produced
by Nothing *at any definite Time* ;
the Ability of Nothing to produce
any thing, being plainly the fame
in Time or in *Eternity.*) And
I have moreover proved *ex abun-*
dantı, in the foregoing part of this
Tenth

Tenth Head, that the Power of Beginning Motion is not only *poſſible* and *certain* in it ſelf, but alſo *poſſible to be communicated* to Finite Beings, and *actually Is* in Man.

That Thinking and Willing, neither are, nor can be Affections of Matter. 2*dly.* Thinking and Willing neither are, nor can be, Qualities or Affections of *Matter*; and conſequently are not concluded under the Laws thereof. That 'tis poſſible there may be Immaterial Subſtances, the Notion not implying a Contradiction in it ſelf, hath already been ſhown under the preſent General Propoſition. Further, that Thinking and Willing are Powers entirely Different from Solidity, Figure, and Motion; and if they be Different, that then they cannot poſſibly ariſe from them, or be compounded of them; hath likewiſe been already proved under the *Eighth* General Head of this

this Discourse. It follows therefore, that Thinking and Willing
may possibly be, nay that they *certainly and necessarily are* Faculties or
Powers of Immaterial Substances:
Seeing they *cannot possibly* be Qualities or Affections of *Matter;* unless we will confound (as some
have done) the Ideas of things;
and mean by *Matter,* not, what
the Word commonly is used to signifie, a Solid Substance, capable
of Division, Figure and Motion;
but an unknown Substance, capable of Powers or Properties entirely different from these: In which
Sense of the Word, could *Matter*
be supposed 'never so capable of
Thinking and Willing; yet in
that Sense, (as I shall show presently) it would signifie nothing
at all, to the Purpose or Advantage of our Adversaries. In the
mean time, how great an Absurdity

ſurdity it is, to ſuppoſe Thinking and Willing to be Qualities
or Affections of *Matter*, in the
Proper and Uſual Senſe of the
Word ; may ſufficiently appear,
without any foreign Argument,
from the Senſeleſneſs of Mr *Hobbs's
Own* Explication of the Nature
and Original of Senſation and
Conſciouſneſs. *The Immediate Cauſe
of Senſation*, * ſaith
he, *is this : The Ob-
ject, or Something flow-
ing from it, preſſeth the
outermoſt part of the
Organ, and that Pres-
ſure is communicated to
the innermoſt Parts of
the Organ ; Where by
the Reſiſtence or Reacti-
on of the Organ, cau-
ſing a Preſſure outwards,
contrary to the Preſſure
of the Object inwards,
there*

* Ex quo intelligi-
tur, Senſionis immedi-
atam cauſam eſſe in eo,
quod Senſionis Orga-
num primum & tangit
& premit. Si enim or-
gani pars extima pre-
matur ; illa cedente,
premetur quoq; pars
quæ verſus interiora illi
proxima eſt ; & ita pro-
pagabitur preſſio, ſive
motus ille, per partes
Organi Omnes, uſq; ad
intimam.————Quo-
niam autem motui ab
objecto per media ad
Organi partem inti-

there *is made up a Phantasm, or Image:* Which *Phantasm,* † saith he, *is the Sensation it self.* Again; *The Cause of Sensation,* ‖ saith he, *is an Object pressing the Organ;* which *Pressure is by means of the Nerves conveyed to the Brain, and so to the Heart;* tanquam aliquid situm extra Organum. *Hobbs de Sensione & motu animali.*

mam propagato, fit aliqua totius Organi resistentia sive reactio, per motum ipsius Organi internum naturalem; fit propterea conatui ab objecto, conatus ab Organo contrarius: Ut cum conatus ille ad intima, ultimus actus fit eorum qui fiunt in actu Sensionis; tum demum ex ea reactione aliquandiu durante, ipsum existit *Phantasma;* quod propter conatum versus externa, semper videtur

† Phantasma est sentiendi Actus: *Id. ibid.*

‖ Causa sensionis est Externum Corpus sive Objectum, quod premit Organum proprium; & premendo, (mediantibus Nervis & Membranis,) continuum efficit Motum introrsum ad Cerebrum & inde ad Cor; unde nascitur Cordis resistentia & contrapressio seu ἀντιτυπία sive Conatus Cordis liberantis se a pressione per motum tendentem extrorsum; qui motus propterea apparet tanquam aliquid externum: Atq, Apparitio hæc, sive Phantasma, est id quod vocamus *Sensionem. Leviathan Cap.* I.

where

where by the Refiftence or Counter-
preffure of the Heart outwards, is
made an Image or Phantafm, which
is Senfation. Now what is there
in all this, that does in any the
leaft meafure tend to explain or
make intelligible the real and
inward Nature of Senfe or Confcioufnefs ? The Object, by com-
municating a Preffure through
the Organ to the Senfory,
does indeed raife a *Phantafm* or I-
mage, that is, make a *certain Im-*
preffion on the Brain : But Wherein
confifts the Power of *Perceiving* this
Impreffion, and of being *Senfible* of
it ? Or what Similitude hath this Impreffion to the *Senfe it felf*, that is,
to the *Thought* excited in the Mind ?
why, exactly the very fame, that
a *Square* has to *Bluenefs*, or a
Triangle to *Sound*, or a *Needle* to
the Senfe of *Pain* ;• or the *Refle-*
cting of a Tennis-Ball, to the *Reafon*
and

and Understanding of a Man. So that Mr. *Hobbs's* Definition of Sensation; that it is it self, the inmost and formal Nature of it, nothing but the Phantasm or Image made in the Brain by the Pressure communicated from the Object; is in other Words, defining *Blueness* to be the Image of a *Square,* or *Sound* the Picture of a *Triangle,* or *Pain* the Similitude of a *Sharp-pointed Needle.* I do not here misrepresent him in the least. For He himself expresly confesses, * that *all Sensible Qualities, such as Colour, Sound and the like, are in the Objects themselves nothing but Motion ; And because Motion can produce Nothing but Motion ,* (as likewise 'tis evident that Figure and

* Quæ qualitates Omnes nominari solent sensibiles, & sunt in ipso objecto nihil aliud præter materiæ motum, quo Objectum in Organa Sensuum diversimode operatur. Neq; in *Nobis* aliud sunt, quam diversi motus. Motus enim nihil generat præter motum. *Leviathan cap.* 1.

all

all its possible Compositions can produce nothing but Figure,) *therefore in* Us *also the Perceptions of these sensible Qualities are nothing but different Motions.*   If then the Phantasm, that is, the Image of the Object made in the Brain by Figure and Motion, be (as he says) the Sensation it self; is not Sensation, bare Figure and Motion? And are not all the forementioned Absurdities, unavoidable Consequences of his Opinion?

Mr. *Hobbs,* (as I have elsewhere observed,) seems indeed not to have been altogether unaware of this insuperable Difficulty; But he industriously indeavours to conceal it from his Readers, and to impose upon them by the ambiguity of the Word *Phantasm.*   Yet for a Reserve, in case he should be too hard pressed, * he gives us a Hint, that possibly

* Scio fuisse Philosophos quosdam, eos-

bly *Senfation may be fomething more*, viz. *a Power of Perception or Confcioufnefs naturally and effentially inherent in all Matter* ; *only that it wants the Organs and Memory of Animals to exprefs its Senfation :* And †
that, as a Man, if he were fuppofed to have no other Senfe but Seeing, and That fo ordered, as that his Eyes

demq; *viros doctos*, qui corpora omnia Senfu prædita effe fuftinuerunt : *Nec video*, fi natura Senfionis in reactione fola collocaretur, *quomodo refutari poffint.* Sed etfi ex reactione etiam corporum aliorum phantafma aliquod nafceretur, illud tamen remoto objecto ftatim ceffaret : Nam nifi ad retinendum Motum impreffum, etiam remoto objecto, apta habeant Organa, ut habent Animalia ; ita tantum fentient, ut nunquam fenfiffe fe recordentur.
——Senfioni ergo, quæ vulgo ita appellatur, neceffario adhæret memoria aliqua, &c *Holbs Phyf cap.* 25. *Sect.* 5.

† Itaq, & Senfioni adhæret proprie dictæ, ut ei aliqua infita fit perpetua phantafmatum varietas ; ita ut alud ib alio difcerni poffit. Si fupponemus enim effe hominem, oculis quidem claris cæterifq; videndi Organis recte fe habentibus compofitum, nullo autem alio fenfu præditum, eumq, ad eandem rem eodem femper colore & fpecie fine ulla vel minima varietate apparentem obverfum effe , mihi certe, quicquid dicant alii, non Videre videretur ———Attonitum effe, & fortaffe Afpectare eum, fed ftupentem dicerem, videre non dicerem : Adeo *Sentire femper idam*, & *Non Sentire*, ad idem recidunt. *Id, Ibid.*

were always immoveably fixed upon
one and the same Object, and That
also unchangeable and without any
the least variety; such a Man could
not properly be said to see, but only to be under an unintelligible kind
of Amazement: So all unorganized
Bodies may possibly have Sensation
or Perception; but because for want
of Organs there is no Variety in it,
neither any Memory or Means of ex-
pressing that Sensation, therefore to
Us it seems as if they had no such
Thing at all. This Opinion, I say,
Mr. *Hobbs* mentions as possible;
But he does it with such Hesitan-
cy, Diffidence and Sparingness,
as shows plainly that he meant it
only as a last Refuge, or rather
Subterfuge, to recur to, when he
should be pressed with the fore
mentioned Absurdities unavoidably
Consequent upon the Supposition
of Sensation being only Figure and
Mo

Motion. And indeed well might he be sparing, and, as it were, Ashamed of this Subterfuge : For it is a Thing altogether as absurd, as even the other Opinion it self, of Thought being mere Motion : For what can be more Ridiculous, than to imagine that Matter is as essentially Conscious, as it is extended ? Will it not follow from that Supposition, that every piece of Matter, being made up of endlessly divisible parts, is made up also of innumerable Consciousnesses and infinite Confusion ? But 'tis a shame to trouble the *Reader* with so much as the mention of any of the Numberless Absurdities following from that Monstrous Supposition. Others therefore, who would make Thinking to be an Affection of *Matter*, and yet are Ashamed to use either of the forementioned ways, Contend that *God*

O 3 by

by his Almighty and Supreme Power indues certain Syftems of Matter with a Faculty of Thinking, according to his own Good Pleafure. But this alfo amounts to Nothing. For either our Idea of *Matter*, is a true Idea, or it is not. If it be a true Idea, that *Matter* is Nothing but a Solid Subftance, capable only of Divifion, Figure and Motion, with the Effects of their feveral Compofitions, as it appears to Us, upon the beft Examination we are able to make of it ; then it is abfolutely Impoffible for Thinking to belong to *Matter*, becaufe Thinking cannot poffibly arife from any Modification or Compofition of any or all of thefe Qualities : But if any Man will fay that our Idea of *Matter* is wrong; and that by *Matter* he will not mean, as other Men do, a Solid Subftance, capable only

ly of Divifion, Figure and Motion, with the Effects of their feveral Compofitions ; but an unknown Subftance, capable of
Thinking and of numberlefs unknown Properties befides , then
he trifles only, in putting an am-
biguous Signification upon the
Word *Matter*, and making it
mean the fame as we mean by *Subftance* : And in that Senfe to fuppofe Thinking or any other A-
ctive Property poffible to be in *Matter*, as fignifying only a Subftance of
which we have no Idea ; would
make Nothing at all to *the prefent* Purpofe in our Adverfaries
Advantage, and is *at leaft Not a
clearer and more Intelligible* way
of Talking, than to Attribute the
fame Properties to an Immaterial
Subftance, and keep the Idea of
Matter and *its* Properties clear and
diftinct. For I affirm,

O 4 3*dly;*

3*dly.* That even supposing (in these Mens confused way) that the Soul was really not a distinct Substance from Body, but that Thinking and Willing could be, and were indeed only Qualities of Affections of *Matter* ; yet even *This* would not at all Affect the present Question about *Liberty*, nor prove Freedom of Will to be an impossible Thing. For, since it has been already demonstrated, that Thinking and Willing cannot possibly be Effects or Compositions of Figure and Motion ; Whosoever will make Thinking and Willing to be Qualities or Affections of *Matter*, must suppose *Matter* capable of certain Properties entirely different from Figure and Motion ; And if it be capable of Properties entirely different from Figure and Motion, then it can never be proved from the Effects of Figure and

Motion

Motion being all Neceſſary, that the Effects of other and totally diſtinct Properties muſt likewiſe be Neceſſary.

Mr *Hobbs* therefore, and his Followers, are guilty of a moſt ſhameful Fallacy in that very Argument, wherein they place their main and chief ſtrength. For, ſuppoſing *Matter* to be capable of Thinking and Willing, they contend that the Soul is mere Matter; and Knowing that the Effects of Figure and Motion muſt needs be all neceſſary, they conclude that the Operations of the Mind muſt All therefore be Neceſſary : That is : When they would prove the Soul *to be* mere *Matter* ; then they ſuppoſe Matter capable, not only of Figure and Motion, but alſo of other unknown Properties : And when they would prove the Will and all other Operations of the

Soul

A ſhameful Fallacy of M.Hobbs and his Followers.

Soul to be *Necessary* ; then they de-
vest Matter again of all its Unknown Properties, and make it
mere Solidity endued only with
Figure and Motion, again. Wherefore, distinguishing their Ambigu-
ous and Confused use of the Word
Matter, they are unavoidably reduced to One of these two Con-
cessions. If by *Matter* they mean
a Solid Substance endued only
with Figure and Motion ; then the
Soul cannot be mere matter ; be-
* *Motus* cause (as Mr. *Hobbs* himself * con-
nihil ge- fesses) Figure and Motion can pro-
nerat
præter duce nothing but Figure and Mo-
Motum tion ; and consequently (as hath
Leviath.
Cap. 1. been before demonstrated) they
can never produce so much as any
Secondary Quality, [*Sound, Colour, and the like,*] much less Thinking and Reasoning : From whence
it follows, that the Soul being
unavoidably something Immaterial,

al, they have no Argument left to prove that it cannot have a *Power of Beginning Motion*, which is a plain Instance of *Liberty*. But if, on the other hand, they will mean by *Matter* an Unknown Substance, capable of Properties totally different from Figure and Motion ; then they must no longer argue against the Possibility of Liberty, from the Effects of Figure and Motion being all unavoidably Necessary ; because Liberty will not consist in the Effects of Figure and Motion, but in those Other Unknown Properties of Matter, which these Men can no more explain or argue about, than about Immaterial Substances. The Truth therefore is, they must needs Suppose Thinking, to be merely an Effect or Composion of Figure and Motion, if they will give any strength to their Arguments.

ments againſt Liberty : And then the
Queſtion will be, not whether God
can make *Matter* think, or no, (for
in that Queſtion they only trifle
with a Word, abuſing the Word
Matter to ſignify *Subſtance* in general ,) but the Queſtion is, whether *Figure and Motion*, in any Compoſition or Diviſion, can poſſible Be
Perception and Thought: which (as has
been before ſaid) is juſt ſuch a Queſtion, as if a Man ſhould ask, whether
it be Poſſible that a *Triangle* ſhould
be a *Sound*, or a Globe a *Colour*.
The Sum is this : If the Soul be an
Immaterial Subſtance, (as it muſt
needs be, if we have any true I-
dea of Matter,) then Mr. *Hobbs's*
Arguments againſt the Poſſibility
of Liberty , drawn all from the
Properties of Matter, are idle and
nothing to the Purpoſe : But if
our Adverſaries will be ſo abſurd
as to contend, that the Soul is nothing

thing but mere *Matter* ; Then either they muft mean by *Matter* an unknown Subftance indued with Active as well as Paffive Properties ; which is confounding and taking away our Idea of *Matter,* and at the fame Time deftroying all their own Arguments againft Liberty, which they have founded wholly on the known Properties of Matter : Or elfe they muft fpeak out, as they mean, that Thinking and Willing are nothing but Effects and Compofitions of Figure and Motion ; which I have already fhown to be a Contradiction in Terms.

There are fome other Arguments againft the Poffibility of *Liberty,* which Men by attempting to anfwer, have made to appear confiderable ; when really they are altogether befide the Queftion. As for Inftance, thofe drawn from

the

the Necessity of the *Will's* being determined by the last *Judgement* of the *Understanding*; And from the Certainty of the *Divine* *Præscience*.

As to the former, *viz*: The *Necessity* of the *Will's* being determined by the last *Judgment* of the *Understanding*: This is only a Necessity upon Supposition; that is to say, a Necessity that a Man should *Will* a Thing, when it is supposed that he *does Will* it; just as if one should affirm, that every thing which Is, is therefore Necessary to Be, because when it Is, it cannot but Be. For the *last Judgment of the Understanding* is nothing else but a Man's final Determining, (after more or less Consideration,) either to Choose or not to Choose a thing; that is, it is the very same with the *Act* of *Volition*. But besides, supposing *the last Judgment of the*

Un-

Understanding was really a different Thing from the *Act of Volition*, and that the One *Neceffarily* produced the other ; yet
this *Neceffity* of a Man's *Willing* to act according to his laft
Judgment, would at moft even upon That Suppofition, be only a
Moral, and not properly a *Natural*
Neceffity ; that is, it would be *no
Neceffity at all*, in the Senfe of the
Oppofers of Liberty. For *Moral
Neceffity*, is evidently confiftent
with the moft perfect *Natural Liberty*. For inftance : A Man entirely
free from all Pain of Body and
Diforder of Mind, judges it un-
reafonable for him to Hurt or Deftroy Himfelf ; and, being under
no Temptation or External Vio-
lence, he *cannot poffibly* Act contrary to this Judgment ; not becaufe he wants a *Natural Power* to
do fo, but becaufe it is abfurd
and

and Mischievous and *morally Impossible* for him to Choose to do it. Which also is the very same Reason, why the most perfect Rational Creatures, Superiour to Men, *Cannot* do Evil; not because they want a *Natural Power* to perform the Material Action; but because it is *Morally Impossible*, that with a Perfect Knowledge of what is Best, and without any Temptation to Evil, their Will should determine it self to Choose to Act Foolishly and Unreasonably. I know, the Opposers of Liberty reply here, that there is no Difference between *Natural* and *Moral* Necessity; a Man free from all Pain of Body and Disorder of Mind, being (they say) under a *Natural* Impossibility of hurting or destroying himself; because neither his *Judgment* nor his *Will*, without some Impulse *External* to Both, for-

can any more poſſibly be determined to any Action, than one Body
can begin to move without being
impelled by another. But this is
forſaking the Argument drawn
from the Neceſſity of the *Will's*
following the *Underſtanding,* and
recurs to the former Argument of
the abſolute Impoſſibility of there
being any where a *Firſt Principle of Motion* at all ; which has
been abundantly anſwered already.

The other Argument which I
ſaid has alſo frequently been urged againſt the Poſſibility of Liberty, is the *Certainty of the Divine Preſcience.* But this alſo
is entirely beſide the Queſtion.
For if there be no *Other* Arguments, by which it can be proved antecedently, That All Actions
are *Neceſſary;* 'Tis certain it can never be made appear to follow from

The Certainty of Divine Fore-knowlege not inconſiſtent with the Liberty of Mens Actions.

Pre-

Præſcience alone, that they muſt be
ſo. That is, if upon *Other Accounts* there be no Impoſſibility,
but that the Actions of Men may
be free ; *the bare Certainty of the
Divine Fore-Knowledge,* can never
be Proved to deſtroy that Freedom : And Conſequently the Certainty of *Præſcience,* ſeparated
from *Other* Arguments, is altogether beſide the Queſtion of Liberty.   As ro the *Other* Arguments, uſually intermingled with
this Queſtion ; They have all, I
think, been anſwered already :
And now that, if upon other accounts there be no Impoſſibility
for the Actions of Men to be free,
the *bare Certainty of the Divine
Fore-Knowledge* can never be proved to deſtroy that Freedom ; is
very Evident. For bare Fore-
knowledge, has no Influence at all
in any Reſpect ; nor affects in any
mea-

meafure the manner of the Exiftence of Any Thing. All that
the greateft Oppofers of Liberty
have ever urged, or can urge, upon this Head, amounts only to
This ; that *Fore-Knowledge* implies
Certainty, and *Certainty* implies *Neceffity.* But Neither is it True,
that *Certainty* implies *Neceffity* ;
neither does *Fore-Knowledge* imply
any other *Certainty,* than fuch a
Certainty only as would be equally
in Things though there was no
Fore-Knowledge.

For (1ft) the *Certainty of Fore-
Knowledge* does not Caufe the *Certainty of Things,* but is it felf
founded on the Reality of their
Exiftence. Whatever Now Is, 'tis
Certain that it is ; and it was ye-
fterday as *certainly* true, that the
Thing *would be* to day, as it is Now
certain that it *Is.* And this *Certainty* of Event is equally the fame,

whether

whether it be suppofed that the Thing could be Fore-known, or not. For whatever at any Time *Is*; it was *certainly* True from E-ternity, as to the Event, that That Thing *would be*: And this Certain Truth of every future Event, would not at all have been the lefs, though there had been no fuch Thing as Fore-Knowledge. Bare Præfcience therefore has no Influence at all upon any Thing; nor contributes in the leaft to-wards the making it Neceffary. We may illuftrate this in fome meafure by the Comparifon of our own Knowledge. We Know cer-tainly that fome Things are; and when we Know that they are, they cannot but Be: Yet 'tis mani-feft our Knowledge does not at all affect the Things to make them more Neceffary or more Certain. Now Fore-Knowledge in God, is the

the very fame as Knowledge. All things are to Him as if they were equally prefent, to all the Pur-pofes of Knowledge and Power. He Knows perfectly every thing that Is : And he fore-knows whatever fhall be, in the fame Manner as he Knows what Is. As therefore Knowledge has no In-fluence on Things that are; fo neither has Fore-knowledge, on Things that fhall be. 'Tis true : the *Manner* how God can forefee Future Things, without a Chain of Neceffary Caufes; is impoffi-ble for us to explain : But fo al-fo are Numberlefs other Things, which yet no Man doubts of the Truth of : And if there were any Strength in this Argument ; it would prove, not againft *Liberty*, but againft *Præfcience* it felf. For if thefe two things were really in-confiftent, and one of them muft

P 3 be

be deſtroyed, the introducing an abſolute and univerſal Fatality, which
evidently deſtroys all Religion and
Morality, would tend more of the
two to the Diſhonour of God, than
denying him a Fore-knowledge,
which upon this Suppoſition
would be impoſſible and imply a
Contradiction to ſuppoſe him to
have. But the Caſe is not thus.
For tho' we cannot indeed explain
the *manner* of God's foreſeeing
the Actions of Free Agents; yet
thus much we know, that the bare
Fore-knowledge of any Action,
that would upon all other Accounts be Free, cannot alter or
diminiſh that Freedom; it being
evident that Fore-knowledge adds
no other Certainty to any thing,
than what it would equally have
though there were no Fore-knowledge. Unleſs therefore we be antecedently certain, that nothing can
poſſibly be free; and that Liberty

ty is in it self abfolutely an Inconfiftent and Contradictory Notion ; (as I have above fhown that it is not :) bare Fore-knowledge, which makes no alteration at all in any thing, will not be in any wife Inconfiftent with Liberty ; how great Difficulty fo ever there may be, in comprehending the *manner* of fuch Foreknowledge. For if Liberty be in it felf poffible ; The bare *Forefight* of a free Action, *before it be done* ; is nothing different (to any Purpofe in the prefent Queftion) from a fimple *Knowledge* of it, *when it is done :* Both thefe Kinds of Knowledge, implying plainly a *Certainty only* of the Event, (which would be the fame tho' there were no fuch Knowledge) and not at all any *Neceffity* of the Thing.

For (*2dly.*) As *Fore-knowledge* implies not any other Certainty,

P 4 than

than such as would be equally in Things though there were *no Fore-knowledge* : So neither does this Certainty of Event, in any sort imply *Necessity.* For, let a Fatalist *suppose,* (what he does *not* yet *grant,*) that there was in Man (as we assert) a Power of Beginning Motion, that is, of acting freely ; and let him suppose further, if he please, that those Actions could not possibly be foreknown : Will there not yet, notwithstanding this Supposition, be in the Nature of things the same *Certainty of Event* in every one of the Man's Actions, as if they were never so Fatal and Necessary ? For Instance : Suppose the Man by an internal Principle of Motion and an Absolute Freedom of Will, without any External Cause or Impulse at all, does some particular Action *to Day* ;

and

and suppose it was not possible that this Action should have been fore-seen *Yesterday* ; was there not nevertheless the same *Certainty of Event*, as if it had been fore-seen ? That is ; would it not, notwithstanding the *supposed* Freedom, have been as *Certain a Truth* Yesterday, that this Action *was* in Event *to be performed to Day* (though supposed never so impossible to have been fore-known,) as it is now a *Certain and Infallible Truth* that it is performed ? Mere *Certainty of Event* therefore, does not in any measure imply *Necessity* : And consequently *Fore-knowledge*, however impossible to be explained as to the *Manner* of it, yet since 'tis evident it implies no other Certainty but only that Certainty of Event which the Thing would equally have without being fore-known,

'tis

'tis evident that *It* alſo implies no Neceſſity.

Of the Original of Evil. And Now having, as I hope, ſufficiently proved both the Poſſibility and the Real Exiſtence of *Liberty* : I ſhall, from what has been ſaid on this Head, draw only this One Inference ; that hereby we are inabled to Anſwer that Antient and Great Queſtion, Πόθεν τὸ κακόν' ; what is the Cauſe and Original of *Evil.* For Liberty implying a *Natural* Power of doing Evil, as well as Good ; and the Imperfect Nature of Finite Beings making it poſſible for them to abuſe that their Liberty to an actual Commiſſion of Evil ; and it being Neceſſary to the Order and Beauty of the Whole, and for diſplaying the Infinite Wiſdom of the Creator, that there ſhould be different and various degrees of Creatures, whereof

whereof consequently some must be *less Perfect* than others; Hence there necessarily arises a Possibility of Evil, notwithstanding that the Creator is infinitely Good. In short, thus: All that we call *Evil*, is either an *Evil of Imperfection*, as the *Want of certain Faculties and Excellencies which other Creatures have*; or *Natural Evil*, as *Pain*, *Death*, and the like; or *Moral Evil*, as all kind of *Vice*. The *First* of these, is not properly an Evil: For every Power, Faculty, or Perfection, which any Creature enjoys, being the Free Gift of God, which he was no more obliged to bestow, than he was to confer Being or Existence it self; 'tis plain, the want of any certain Faculty or Perfection in any Kind of Creatures, which never belonged to their Nature, is no more an Evil to Them, than their

their never having been Created
or brought into Being at all,
could properly have been called
an Evil.   The *Second* Kind of E-
vil, which we call Natural Evil,
is either a Neceſſary Conſequence
of the former , as *Death*, to a
Creature on whoſe Nature Im-
mortality was never conferred ,
and then 'tis no more properly an
Evil, than the Former : Or elſe
it is counterpoiſed in the whole
with as Great or Greater Good ;
as the *Afflictions and Sufferings of
Good Men* ; and then alſo it is not
properly an Evil : Or elſe laſtly
'tis a *Puniſhment* ; and then 'tis a
Neceſſary Conſequent of the *Third*
and laſt ſort of Evil, viz. *Moral
Evil* : And this ariſes wholly from
the abuſe of *Liberty*; which God
gave to his Creatures for other Pur-
poſes, and which 'twas reaſonable
and fit to give them for the Perfection

on and Order of the whole Creation ; Only they, contrary to
Gods Intention and Command,
have abufed what was Neceffary
for the Perfection of the whole,
to the Corruption and Depravation of themfelves ; And thus all
Sorts of Evils have entred into the
World, without any Diminution to the infinite Goodnefs of the
Creator and Governour thereof.

XI. *The Supreme Caufe and Au-thor of all Things, muft of Neceffity be infinitely Wife.* This Propofition is evidently Confequent upon
thofe that have already been proved ; and They being eftablifhed,
This, as admitting no further Dif-
pute, needs not to be largely infifted upon. For nothing is more
evident, than that an *Infinite, Om-
niprefent, Intelligent Being,* muft
Know

That the Supreme Caufe of allThings muft be infinitely Wife.

Know perfectly *all things that Are*; and that, He who alone is *Self-existent and Eternal*, *the Sole Cause and Author of all Things*; *from whom alone all the Powers of all Things are derived*, *and on whom they continually depend*; must also Know perfectly all those Powers, that is, *all Possibilities of Things to come*, and what in every respect is Best and Wisest to be done; and having Infinite *Power*, can never be controuled or prevented from doing what he so knows to be Fittest: From all which, it manifestly follows, that every Effect of the Supreme Cause, must be the Product of Infinite Wisdom. More particularly: The Supreme Being, because he is *Infinite*, must be every where present: And because he is an Infinite *Mind* or *Intelligence*; therefore where-ever he Is, his Knowledge Is, which is inseparаfeparable from his Being, and muft therefore be infinite likewife : And where ever his Infinite Knowledge is, it muft neceffarily have a *full and perfect* Profpect of all things, and nothing can be concealed from its Infpection : He includes and furrounds every thing with his boundlefs Prefence; and penetrates every part of their Subftance with his All-feeing Eye : So that the inmoft Nature and Effence of all things, are perfectly Naked and Open to his View; and even the deepeft Thoughts of Intelligent Beings themfelves, manifeft in his fight. Further, All Things being not only prefent to him, but alfo entirely *Depending* upon him; and having *received* both their Being it felf, and all their Powers and Faculties *from Him*; 'tis manifeft that, as he knows all things that *are*, fo he

muft

muſt likewiſe know all Poſſibilities of Things, that is, All Effects that *Can be.* For, being him-ſelf only Self-Exiſtent, and having Alone *given* to all Things all the Powers and Faculties they are indued with ; 'tis evident He muſt of Neceſſity know perfectly, what All and Each of thoſe Pow-ers and Faculties, which are *deri-ved wholly from himſelf,* can poſſi-bly Produce : And Seeing at one boundleſs View, all the Poſſible Compoſitions and Diviſions, Va-riations and Changes, Circumſtan-ces and Dependencies of Things , all their poſſible Relations one to another, and Diſpoſitions or Fit-neſſes to certain and reſpective Ends ; He muſt without Poſſibility of Error, know exactly what is Beſt and Popereſt in every one of the Infinite Poſſible Caſes or Methods of Diſpoſing Things ; and undei-
ſtand

ftand perfectly how to Order and Direct the refpective Means, to bring about what he fo knows to be in its Kind or in the Whole the Beft and Fitteft in the End. This is what we mean by *Infinite Wif-dom.* And having before fhown, (which indeed is alfo Evident of it felf,) that the Supreme Caufe is moreover *All Powerful* ; fo that He can no more be Prevented by Force or Oppofition, than he can be hindred by Error or Miftake, from *Effecting* always what is abfolutely Fitteft and Wifeft to be done : It follows undeniably that he is *actually and effectually,* in the Higheft and moft complete Senfe, *Infinitely Wife* ; and that the World, and all Things therein, muft be and are Effects of Infinite Wifdom. This is Demonftration *a priori.* The Proof *a pofteriori,* of the Infinite Wifdom

Q   of

of God, from the Confideration
of the Exquisite Perfection and
Consummate Excellency of his
Works, is no less strong and undeniable: But I shall not inlarge
upon this Argument; because it
has frequently already been accurately and strongly urged, to the
everlasting shame and confusion of
Atheists, by the ablest and learn-
edest Writers both of Antient and
Modern Times. I shall here observe only this One Thing : That
the Older the World grows, and
the deeper Men inquire into
Things, and the more Accurate
Observations they make, and the
more and greater Discoveries they
find out ; the stronger this Argument continually grows : Which
is a certain Evidence of its being
founded in Truth. If *Galen* so
many Ages ago, could find in the
Construction and Constitution of

the

the parts of a Humane Body, ſuch undeniable marks of Contrivance and Deſign; as forced him *Then* to acknowledge and Admire the Wiſdom of its Author: What would he have ſaid, if he had known the *Late* Diſcoveries in Anatomy and Phyſick, the Circulation of the Blood, the exact Structure of the Heart and Brain, the Uſes of Numberleſs Glands and Valves for the Secretion and Motion of the Juices in the Body, beſides ſeveral Veins and other Veſſels and Receptacles not at all known, or imagined ſo much as to have any Exiſtence, *in his Days*; but which *Now* are diſcovered to ſerve the Wiſeſt and moſt exquiſite Ends imaginable? If the Arguments againſt the Belief of the Being of an All-wiſe Creator and Governor of the World, which *Epicurus* and his Follower *Lucretius* drew from the

Faults

Faults which they imagined they
could Find in the Frame and Constitution of the *Earth*, were so
Poor and Inconsiderable, that
even in that Infancy of Natural
Philosophy the Generality of
Men, contemned and despised
them as of no force : How
would they have been ashamed, if they had lived in these
Days ; when those very things,
which they thought to be Faults
and Blunders in the Constitution
of Things, are discovered to be
very useful and of exceeding Benefit to the Preservation and Well-
Being of the whole ? And, to
mention no more : If *Tully*, from
the partial and very imperfect
Knowlege in Astronomy, which
His Times afforded, could be
so confident of the Heavenly
Bodies being Disposed and Moved
by a Wise and Understanding
Mind

Mind, as to Declare, that in his Opinion, whoever afferted the contrary, was himfelf *

Void of all Under-ftanding: What wou'd He have faid, if he had know the *Modern* Difcoveries in Aftro-nomy ? The *Immenfe Greatneß* of the World; (I mean of that Part of it, which falls under our Ob-fervation ;) which is Now known to be as much Greater than what in his Time they imagined it to Be, as the World it felf, accord-ing to their Syftem, was Greater than *Archimedes*'s Sphere ? The *Exquifite Regularity* of all the Planets Motions, without Epicycles, Stati-ons, Retrogradations, or any other Deviation or Confufion whatfo-ever? The *inexpreffible Nicety* of the Adjuftment of the Primary

* Cæleftem ergo admi-rabilem ordinem in-credibilemque conftan-tiäm, ex qua confer-vatio & falus omnium omnis oritur, qui va-care mente putat, is ipfe mentis expers ha-bendus eft. *De Natu-ra Deorum, lib.* 2.

Velo-

Velocity and Original Direction of the *Annual* Motion of the Planets, with their Distance from the Central Body and their force of Gravitation towards it ? The *wonderful Proportion* of the *Diurnal* Motion of the Earth and other Planets about their own Centers; for the Distinction of Light and Darkness, without that monstrously disproportionate Whirling of the whole Heavens, which the Antient Astronomers were forced to suppose ? The *exact Accommodating* the * *Densities* of the Planets, to their Distances from the Sun, and consequently to the Proportion of Heat which each of them is to bear respectively ; so that

* Planetarum *densitates* fere funt, ut radices diametrorum apparentium applicatæ ad diametros veras, hoc eft, reciproce ut diftantiæ Planetarum a fole, ductæ in radices diametrorum apparentium. Collocavit igitur Deus Planetas in diverfis diftantiis a fole, ut *quilibet pro gradu denfitatis, calore folis majore vel minore fruatur*. Newton. Princip. *Lib.* 3; *Prop.* 8.

neither

neither Thofe which are neareft to the Sun, arc deftroyed by the Heat ; nor Thofe which are fartheft off, by the Cold; but each one enjoys a Temperature fuited to its proper Ufes, as the Earth is to ours ? The *Admirable Order, Number and Ufefulneß,* of the feveral *Moons,* (as I may very properly call them,) never dreamt of by Antiquity, but Now by the Help of Telefcopes *clearly and diftinctly feen* to move about their refpective Planets; and whofe Motions are fo actly Known, that their very Eclipfes are as certainly calculated and foretold, as thofe of our own Moon ? The *ftrange Adjuftment of our* Moon's *Motion about its own Center* once in a Month, with its Motion about the Earth in the fame Period of Time, to fuch a degree of Exactnefs, that *by that*

Q 4 *means*

means the same Face is always Obverted to the Earth without any Sensible Variation ? What, I say, would *Tully*, that great Master of Reason, have thought and said, if these and other Newly Discovered Instances of the Unexpressible Accuracy and Wisdom of the Works of God, had been found out and Known in *His* Time ? Certainly Atheism, which *Then* was infinitely unable to withstand the Arguments drawn from this Topick ; must *Now*, upon the additional Strength of these later Observations, which are every one an unanswerable Proof of the incomprehensible Wisdom of the Creator, be utterly ashamed to show its Head. We *Now* see with how great reason the Author of the Book of *Ecclesiasticus*, after he had described the Beauty

of

of the Sun and Stars, and all the then Vifible Works of God in Heaven and Earth, conluded, *ch.* 43, *v.* 32, (as *We* after all the Difcoveries of later Ages, may no doubt ftill truly fay,) *There are yet hid greater things than thefe, and we have feen but a few of his Works.*

XII. Laftly, *The Supreme Caufe and Author of all Things, muft of Neceffity be a Being of Infinite Goodnefs, Juftice and Truth, and all other Moral Perfections ; fuch as Become the Supreme Governour and Judge of the World.* That there are *different Relations* of Things one towards another, is as certain as that there are *Different Things* in the World : That from thefe *Different Relations of Different Things,*

The Supreme Author of all Things muft be infinitely Good, Juft and True.

Things, there neceffarily arifes an *Agreement* or *Difagreement* of fome Things to others, or a *Fitnefs* or *Unfitnefs* of the Application of Different Things or Different Re-lations one to another ; is like-wife as certain, as that there is any Difference in the Nature of Things, or that Different Things do Exift. Further, that there is a *Fitnefs* or *Suitablenefs* of certain *Circumftances* to certain *Perfons,* and an *Unfuitablenefs* of Others, Founded in the *Nature of Things* and the *Qualifications of Perfons,* antecedent to *Will* and to all *Ar-bitrary* or *Pofitive Appointment whatfoever* ; muft unavoidably be acknowledged by every one, who will not affirm that 'tis *equally Fit and Suitable,* in the *Nature and Reafon of Things,* that an Innocent Being fhould be *extremely and eter-nally*

nally Miserable, as that it should
be Free from such Misery. There
is therefore such a Thing as *Fitness* and *Unfitness,* eternally, necessarily and unchangeably, in the
Nature and Reason of Things.
Now what these *Relations of
Things* absolutely and Necessarily
Are in Themselves; That also they
Appear to be, to the Understanding
of all Intelligent Beings; except
Those only, who Understand
Things to Be what they Are not,
that is, whose Understandings are
either very imperfect or very depraved. And by this *Understanding or Knowledge* of the Natural
and Necessary Relations of Things,
the *Actions likewise* of all Intelligent Beings are constantly Directed; (which *by the by* is the
true Ground and Foundation of
all Morality :) unless their *Will*
be

be corrupted by particular *Interest or Affection*, or fwayed by fome unreafonable and prevailing Luft. The Supreme Caufe therefore, and Author of all Things ; fince (as has already been Proved) he muft of neceffity have Infinite *Knowledge*, and the Perfection of *Wifdom* ; fo that 'tis abfolutely impoffible he fhould *Err* or be in any refpect *Ignorant* of the True Relations and Fitnefs or Unfitnefs of Things, or be by any means *Deceived* or Impofed upon herein : And fince he is likewife *Self-Exiftent*, Abfolutely *Independent* and *All-Powerful*; fo that, having no *want* of any thing, 'tis impoffible his *Will* fhould be influenced by any wrong *Affection*; and, having no Dependence, 'tis impoffible his *Power* fhould be limited by any Superiour Strength : 'Tis evident He

must

muſt of Neceſſity (meaning, not a *Neceſſity of Fate*, but ſuch a *Moral Neceſſity* as I before ſaid was conſiſtent with the moſt perfect Liberty,) *Do* always what he *Knows* to be *Fitteſt to be Done :* that is, He muſt Act always according to the ſtricteſt Rules of Infinite *Goodneſs, Juſtice* and *Truth*, and all other *Moral Perfections.* In Particular ; The Supreme Cauſe muſt in the firſt place be infinitely *Good* ; that is, he muſt have an unalterable Diſpoſition to *Do* and to *Communicate* Good or Happineſs : Becauſe being Himſelf neceſſarily *Happy* in the Eternal injoyment of his own Infinite Perfections, he cannot poſſibly have any other Motives to make any Creatures at all, but only that He may Communicate to Them His Own Perfections ; according

cording to their *different Capacities,* arising from that *Variety of Natures,* which it was Fit for *Infinite Wisdom* to produce ; and according to their *different Improvements,* arising from that *Liberty,* which is essentially Necessary to the Constitution of *Intelligent and Active Beings.* That he must be Infinitely *Good,* appears likewise further from hence ; that being Necessarily *All-Sufficient,* he must consequently be infinitely removed from all *Malice* and *Envy,* and from all other Possible Causes or Temptations of doing Evil ; which, it is evident, can only be Effects of *Want and Weakness,* of *Imperfection* or *Depravation.* Again ; The Supreme Cause and Author of all things, must in like manner be infinitely *Just* ; Because the *Rule of Equity* being no-

nothing elfe but the *Very Nature*
of Things, and their *neceffary Relations* one to Another ; and the
Execution of Juftice, being nothing elfe but a fuiting the *Circumftances of Things* to the *Qualifications of Perfons*, according to
that Original *Fitnefs and Agreea-
blenefs*, which I have before
fhown to be *Neceffarily in Nature*,
Antecedent to *Will and all Pofitive Appointment* ; 'Tis evident
that He who *Knows perfectly* this
Rule of Equity, and neceffarily
Judges of Things as they Are ;
who has *complete Power* to Exe-
cute Juftice according to that
Knowledge, and *No poffible Temptation* to deviate in the leaft there-
from ; who can neither be *impofed upon* by any *Deceit*, nor *fwayed* by any *Byafs*, nor *awed* by any
Power ; muft of Neceffity do always

ways that which is *Right* ; without Iniquity, and without Partiality ; without Prejudice, and without Refpect of Perfons. Laftly ; That the Supreme Caufe and Author of all things, muft be *True* and *Faithful*, in all his *Declarations* and all his *Promifes* ; is moft evident: For the only Poffible Reafon of Falfifying, is either *Rafhnefs* or *Forgetfulnefs*, *Inconftancy* or *Impotency*, *Fear of Evil* or *Hope of Gain* : From * all which, an infinitely *Wife*, *All-fufficient* and *Good* Being, muft of Neceffity be infinitely removed; and confequently, as it is impoffible for him *to be deceived himfelf*, fo * neither is it poffible for Him in any wife *to deceive* Others.   In a Word !

++ 'Ουκ ἔςιν ᾧ ἕιεκα ἀν θεὸς ψεύδοιτο — Κομιδῇ ἄρα ὁ θεὸς ἀπλῶι ἢ ἀληθὲς, ἔν τε ἔργω ἢ ἐν λόγω. Καὶ ἔτε αὐτὸς μεθίςαται, ἔτε ἄλλες ἐξαπατᾷ, ἔτε κατὰ φαντασίας, ἔτε κατὰ λόγες, ἔτε κατὰ σημεί͂ων πομπὰς, ἔθ' ὕπαρ ἐδ' ὄναρ. *Plato de Repub. Lib.* 2. *Sub finem.*

Word : All Evil and All Imperfection whatsoever, arise plainly either from *Shortness of Understanding, Defect of Power,* or *Faultiness of Will* ; and this last, evidently from some *Impotency, Corruption* or *Depravation* ; being nothing else, but a direct Choosing to Act contrary to the known Reason and Nature of Things : From all which, it being manifest that the Supreme Cause and Author of all Things, cannot but be infinitely Removed ; It follows undeniably, that he must of Necessity be *a Being of Infinite Goodness, Justice and Truth, and all other Moral Perfections.*

To this Argumentation *a priori,* there can be opposed but one Objection that I know of, drawn on the contrary *a posteriori,* from Experience and Observation of the Unequal Distributions of Providence

R   dence

dence in the World. But (besides the juft Vindication of the
Wifdom and Goodnefs of Providence in its Difpenfations even
with refpect to this prefent World
only, which *Plutarch* and other Hea-
then Writers have judicioufly made)
the Objection it felf is entirely
wide of the Queftion. For concerning the Juftice and Goodnefs
of God, (as of any Governour
whatfoever,) no Judgment is to
be made from a partial View
of a few fmall Portions of his
Difpenfations, but from an En-
tire Confideration of the Whole;
and confequently not only the
fhort Duration of this prefent
State, but moreover All that is
paft and that is ftill to come,
muft be taken into the Obfervation : and Then every thing will
clearly appear juft and right.

From this Account of the Moral

ıal Attributes of God, it follows,

1st. That though All the Acti- *The Ne-*
ons of God, are entirely Free ; *cessity of*
Gods
and consequently the Exercise of *Moral*
his Moral Attributes cannot be said *Attri-*
butes con-
to be Necessary, in the same Sense *sistent*
of Necessity as his Existence and *with per-*
fect Li-
Eternity are Necessary ; yet these *berty.*
Moral Attributes are *really and tru-*
ly Necessary, by such a Necessity,
as, though it be not at all inconsistent with Liberty, yet is equally Certain, Infallible, and to be
Depended upon, as even the Existence it self, or the Eternity of
God. For though nothing is more
Certain (*as has been already Pro-*
ved in the Ninth Proposition of this
Discourse) than that God Acts,
not necessarily, but *voluntarily,* with
particular intention and design,
knowing that he does Good, and
intending to do so, freely and
out of choice, and when he has

no

no other conftraint upon him but this, that his Goodnefs inclines his Will to communicate himfelf and to do Good, fo that the Divine Nature is under no Neceffity, but fuch as is confiftent with the moft perfect Liberty and Freeft Choice : (which is the Ground of all our Prayers and Thankfgivings :) yet it is neverthelefs as *truly and abfolutely impoffible* for God not to do (or to do any thing contrary to,) what his Moral Attributes require him to do; as if he was really, not a Free, but a Neceffary Agent. And the Reafon hereof, is plain : Becaufe Infinite Knowledge, Power, and Goodnefs in Conjunction, may, notwithftanding the moft perfect Freedom and Choice, Act with altogether as much *Certainty and Unalterable Steddinefs* ; as even the Neceffity of Fate can be fuppofed to do : Nay they cannot poffibly

but

but fo Act; becaufe Free Choice
in a Being of Infinite Knowledge,
Power, and Goodnefs, can no more
Choofe to Act contrary to thefe
Perfections; than *Knowledge* can
be *Ignorance, Power* be *Weaknefs,* or
Goodnefs Malice; So that *Free Choice,*
in fuch a Being, may be as *Certain*
a Principle of Action, as the Neceffity of Fate. We may therefore as certainly and infallibly rely
upon the *Moral,* as upon the *Natural* Attributes of God : It being as abfolutely impoffible for
Him to Act contrary to the One,
as to Deveft himfelf of the Other;
And as much a Contradiction,
to fuppofe him choofing to Do
any thing inconfiftent with his
Juftice, Goodnefs and Truth; as
to fuppofe him devefted of Infinity, Power, or Exiftence. The
One is contrary to the *Immediate
and Abfolute Neceffity of his Nature*;

R 3 The

The other to the unalterable *Rectitude of his Will*: The One is in it self an *Immediate Contradiction in the Terms*; The other is an ex-*press Contradiction to the Necessary Perfections of the Divine Nature*: To suppose the One, is saying absolutely that *Something Is at the same Time that it is not*: To suppose the Other, is saying that *Infinite Knowledge* can Act *Ignorantly*, *Infinite Power Weakly*, or that Infinite *Wisdom and Goodness* can Do Things *Not Good or Wise to be done*. All which, are *equally Great*, and *equally Manifest* Absurdities. This I humbly conceive, is a very Intelligible Account of the Moral Attributes of God ; satisfactory to the Mind, and without Perplexity and Confusion of Ideas. I might have said it at once, (as the Truth most certainly is,) that Justice, Goodness, and all the other Moral

Attri-

Attributes of God, are as *Essen-tial* to the Divine Nature, as the Natural Attributes of Eternity, Infinity, and the like. But because all Atheistical Persons, after they are fully convinced that there must needs be in the Universe some one Eternal, Necessary, Infinite, and All-powerful Being; will still with unreasonable Obstinacy contend, that they can by no means see any necessary Connexion of Goodness, Justice, or any other Moral Attribute, with these Natural Perfections: Therefore I chose to indeavour to Demonstrate the Moral Attributes by a particular Deduction, in the manner I have now Done.

2*dly.* From hence it follows, that though God is a most perfectly free Agent, yet he cannot but do always what is Best and Wisest in the whole. The Reason is evident : Because Perfect Wis-

Of the Necessity of God's doing always what is Best and Fittest i the whole

Wisdom and Goodness, are as *Steddy and Certain* Principles of Action, as Necessity it self : And an Infinitely Wise and Good Being, indued with the most perfect Liberty, can no more Choose to act in contradiction to Wisdom and Goodness ; than a Necessary Being can Act contrary to the Necessity, by which it is acted : It being as great an Absurdity and Impossibility *in Choice,* for Infinite Wisdom to choose to act Unwisely, or Infinite Goodness to choose what is not Good ; as it is in *Nature,* for absolute Necessity to fail of producing its necessary Effect. There was indeed no *Necessity in Nature,* that God should at first Create such Beings as he has Created, or indeed any Being at all ; because He is in Himself infinitely Happy ; and All-sufficient : There was also no *Necessity in Nature* that he should

preserve

preferve and continue Things in Being, after they were created; becaufe He would be as Self-fufficient without their Continuance, as he was before their Creation: But it was Fit, and Wife, and Good, that Infinite Wifdom fhould Manifeft, and Infinite Goodnefs Communicate it felf: And therefore it was *Neceffary* (*in the Senfe of Neceffity I am now fpeaking of*) that Things fhould be made at fuch Time, and continued fo long, and indued with various Perfections in fuch Degrees, as Infinite Wifdom and Goodnefs faw it Wifeft and Beft that they fhould be: And *when* and *whilft* Things are in Being, the fame Moral Perfections make it Neceffary, that they fhould be difpofed and governed according to the exacteft and moft unchangeable Laws of Eternal Juftice, Goodnefs and Truth;

Truth ; Becaufe while *Things* and their *feveral Relations* are, they cannot but be what they are ; and an infinitely Wife Being, cannot but know them to be what they are, and judge always rightly concerning the feveral Fitneffes or Unfitneffes of them ; and an infinitely Good Being, cannot but choofe to act always according to this Knowledge of the refpective Fitnefs of Things : It being as truly impoffible for fuch a *Free Agent*, as is abfolutely incapable of being Deceived or Depraved, *to Choofe*, by acting contrary to thefe Laws, to deftroy its own *Perfections* ; as for *Neceffary Exiftence to be able to* deftroy its own *Being*.

*Of the
Impoffibi-
lity of his
doing E-
vil.*   3*dly*. From hence it follows, that though God is both Perfectly Free, and alfo Infinitely Powerful, yet he cannot Poffibly Do any Thing that is Evil.   The Reafon

son of this also is Evident. Because, as 'tis manifest Infinite Power cannot Extend to Natural Contradictions, which imply a Destruction of that very Power, by which they must be supposed to be wrought; so neither can it Extend to Moral Contradictions, which imply a Destruction of some other Attributes, as necessarily belonging to the Divine Nature, as Power. I have already shown, that Justice, Goodness and Truth, are necessarily in God; even as necessarily, as Power and Understanding, and Knowledge of the Nature of Things: 'Tis therefore as Impossible and Contradictory, to suppose *his Will should Choose* to Do any thing contrary to Justice, Goodness or Truth; as that *his Power should be Able* to Do any thing inconsistent with Power. 'Tis no Diminution of Power, not to be

able

able to Do things which are no Object of Power : And 'tis in like manner no Diminution either of Power or Liberty, to have such a Perfect and Unalterable Rectitude of Will, as never Possibly to Choose to do any thing inconsistent with that Rectitude.

That Liberty is not in it self an Imperfection, but a Perfection.

4*thly*. From hence it follows, that Liberty, properly speaking, is not in it self an Imperfection, but a Perfection. For it is in the highest and completest degree, in *God Himself*; Every Act, wherein he Exercises any Moral Attribute, as Goodness, Justice or Truth, proceeding from the most Perfect Liberty and Freest Choice , without which, Goodness would not be Goodness, nor Justice and Truth any Excellencies ; these things, in the very Idea and Formal Notion of them, utterly excluding All Necessity. It has indeed

deed been commonly taught, that
Liberty is a great Imperfection;
becaufe it is the Occafion of all
Sin, and Mifery : But, if we will
fpeak properly, 'tis not Liberty
that expofes us to Mifery,
but only the Abufe of Liberty. 'Tis True; Liberty makes
Men capable of Sin, and confequently liable to Mifery ; neither
of which they could poffibly be,
without Liberty : But he that
will fay every thing is an Imperfection, by the Abufe of which a
Creatuie may become more un-
happy, than if God had never given it that Thing at all ; muft
fay that a Stone is a more excellent and perfect Creature than
Man, becaufe it is not capable of
making it felf miferable, as Man
is : And by the fame Argument,
Reafon and Knowledge, and every other Perfection, nay even Exiftence

stence it self, will be Proved to be an Imperfection; becaufe it is That without which a Creature could not be miferable. The Truth therefore is; The Abufe of Liberty, that is, the Corruption and Depravation of That, without which no Creatures could be happy, is the alone Caufe of their Mifery: But as for Liberty it felf, it is a great Perfection: And the more Perfect any Creature is, the more Perfect is its Liberty: And the Perfecteft Liberty of all, is fuch a Liberty, as can never by any Ignorance, Deceit or Corruption, be byaffed or diverted *Of the* from Choofing, what is the Pro- *higheft* per Object of Free Choice, the *Moral* *Perfecti-* greateft Good.

ons of 5*thly.* From hence it follows, *Rational* *Crea-* that though probably no Rational *tures not* Creature can be in a ftrict Philo- *excluding* *Natural* fophical Senfe *Impeccable*; yet we *Liberty.*   may

may eafily conceive, how God can place fuch Creatures, as he judges worthy of fo Excellent a Gift, in fuch a State of Knowledge and near Communion with himfelf, where Goodnefs and Holinefs fhall appear fo amiable, and where they fhall be exempt from all means of Temptation and Corruption; that it fhall never be poffible for them, notwithftanding the Natural Liberty of their Will, to be feduced from their unchangeable Happinefs in the Everlafting Choice and Enjoyment of their greateft Good : Which is the State of Good Angels, and of the Saints in Heaven.

Laftly, from what has been faid upon this Head, it follows, that the true Ground and Foundation of all Eternal Moral Obligations, is this, that the fame Reafons, *viz:* the forementioned neceffary

That the Grounds of all Moral Obligations are eternal and neceffary, and depend not on any Laws.

and eternal *Different Relations*
which *Different Things* bear one to
another; and the confequent *Fitnefs* or *Unfitnefs* of the Application of different Things or different Relations one to another, unavoidably arifing from that Difference of the Things themfelves;
thefe fame Reafons, I fay, which
always and neceffarily *do* determine
the Will of God, as hath been
before fhown, *ought* alfo conftant-
ly to determine the Will of all
Subordinate Intelligent Beings;
And when they do not, then fuch
Beings Setting up their own unreafonable Self-Will in oppofition to
the Nature and Reafon of Things,
endeavour (as much as in them
lies) to make Things be what they
are not and cannot be, which is
the higheft Prefumption and greateft Infolence imaginable, an acting contrary to their own Reafon
and

and Knowledge ; an attempting to deftroy that Order
by which the Univerfe Subfifts ;
and alfo by confequence an offer-
ing the higheft affront imaginable
to the Creatour of all Things, who
himfelf governs all his Actions by
thefe Rules, and cannot but require
the fame of all his reafonable Creatures. They who found all Moral
Obligations ultimately in the *Will* of
God, muft recur at length to the
fame thing ; only with this difference, that they do not clearly
explain how the Nature and Will
of God himfelf muft be neceffarily Good and Juft, as I have endeavoured to do. They who
found all Moral Obligation only
upon *Laws* made for the good of
Societies, hold an Opinion which
(befides that it is fully confuted
by what has been already faid concerning the eternal and neceffary

S   Difference

Difference of Things,) is moreover fo directly and manifeftly contradictory and inconfiftent with
it felf, that it feems ftrange it
fhould not have been more commonly taken notice of. For if
there be no difference between
Good and Evil, antecedent to all
Laws ; thcre can be no reafon
given why any Laws fhould be
made at all, when all things are
naturally indifferent. To fay that
Laws are neceffary to be made for
the good of Mankind, is confeffing
that certain things tend to the
good of Mankind, that is, to the
preferving and perfecting their
Nature ; which wife Men *there-*
fore think neceffary to be eftablifhed by Laws : And if the reafon
why certain things are eftablifhed
by wife and good Laws, is becaufe thofe things tend to the good
of Mankind ; 'tis manifeft they
were

were good, antecedent to their being confirmed by Laws : Otherwife, if they were not good, antecedent to all Laws; 'tis evident
there could be no reafon why
fuch Laws fhould be made, rather
than the contrary : Which is the
greateft abfurdity in the World.

A ND now, from what has *The Con-*
been faid upon this Argu- *clufion.*
ment, I hope it is in the whole
fufficiently clear, that the Being
and Attributes of God, are to at-
tentive and confidering Minds,
abundantly capable of juft
Proof and Demonftration ; and
that the Adverfaries of God and
Religion, have not *Reafon* on their
fide, (to which they would pretend to be ftrict Adherers,) but
merely vain Confidence, and great
Blindnefs and Prejudice ; when
they

they would have it be thought, that in the Fabrick of the World God has left himself wholly without Witness; and that all the Arguments of Nature, are on the side of Atheism and Irreligion. Some Men, I know, there are, who having never turned their Thoughts to Matters of this Nature, Think that these Things are all absolutely above our Comprehension; and that we Talk about we know not what, when we dispute about these Questions: But since the most considerable Atheists that ever appeared in the World, and the Pleaders for Universal Fatality, have all thought fit to argue in this Way, in their Attempts to remove the first Foundations of Religion; it is Reasonable and Necessary that they should be opposed in their own Way, it being most certain, that no Argumentation,

tation, of what kind foever, can poffibly be made ufe of on the fide of Errour, but may alfo be ufed with much greater Advantage, on the behalf of Truth.

2. From what has been faid on this Argument, we may fee how it comes to pafs, that though nothing is fo certain and undeniable, as the Neceffary Exiftence of God, and the Confequent Deduction of all his Attributes ; yet Men, who have never attended to the Evidence of Reafon and the Notices that God hath given us of Himfelf, may Eafily be in great meafure ignorant of Both. That the three Angles of a Triangle are Equal to two right ones, is fo certain and evident, that whoever affirms the contrary, affirms what may very eafily be reduced to an Exprefs Contradiction : yet whoever bend not their Minds to confider

sider it at all, may easily be ignorant of this and numberless other
the like Mathematical and most infallible Truths.

3. Yet the Notices that God
has been pleased to give us of himself, are so many and so obvious;
in the Constitution, Order, Beauty and Harmony of the several
Parts of the World; in the Frame
and Structure of our own Bodies,
and the wonderful Powers and
Faculties of our Souls; in the unavoidable Apprehensions of our
own Minds, and the common
Consent of all other Men; in
every thing within us, and every
thing without us; that no Man
of the meanest Capacity and greatest Disadvantages whatsoever,
with the slightest and most super-
ficial Observation of the Works
of God, and the lowest and most
obvious attendance to the Reason
of

of Things, can be ignorant of *Him*, but he muft be utterly with-out excufe. He may not indeed be able to underftand or be affect-ed by Nice and Metaphyfical De-monftiations of the Being and Attributes of God : But then for the fame Reafon, he is ob-liged alfo not to fuffer himfelf to be fhaken and unfettled, by the fubtle Sophiftries of Sceptical and Atheiftical Men ; which he cannot perhaps anfwer, becaufe he cannot underftand ; But he is bound to adhere to thofe Things which he knows, and thofe Reafonings he is capable to judge of ; which are abundantly fufficient to determine and to guide the Practice of fober and confidering Men.

4. But this is not all. God has moreover finally, by a clear and exprefs Revelation of Him-felf, brought down from Heaven
by

by his own Son, our Bleſſed Lord and Redeemer, and ſuited to every Capacity and Underſtanding; put to Silence the Ignorance of Fooliſh, and the Vanity of Sceptical and Profane Men: and by Declaring to us Himſelf his own Nature and Attributes, has effectually prevented all Miſtakes, which the Weakneſs of our Reaſon, the Negligence of our Application, the Corruption of our Nature, or the Falſe Philoſophy of wicked and Profane Men, might have led us into; and ſo has infallibly furniſhed us with ſufficient Knowledge, to enable us to perform our Duty in this Life, and to obtain our Happineſs in that which is to come. But this exceeds the Bounds of my preſent Subject, and deſerves to be handled in a particular Diſcourſe.

F